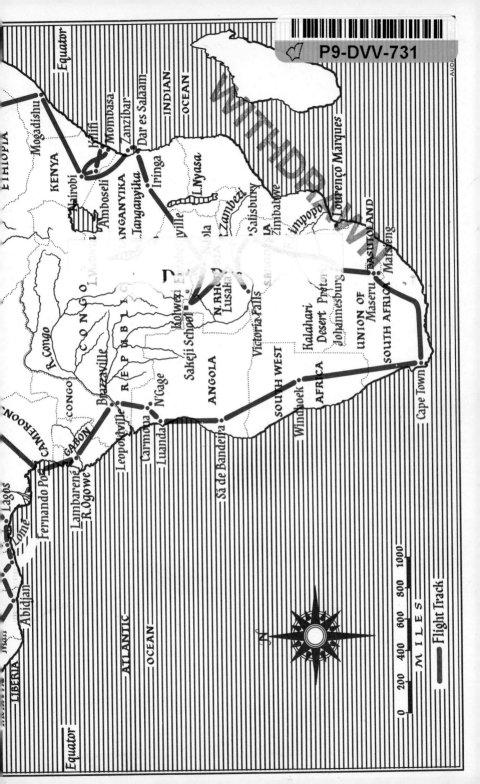

FIRST JOURNEY

FIRST
JOURNEY

Winston S. Churchill

Random House   New York

Acknowledgements are due to the following for permission to quote copyright material:

Odhams Books Ltd and Charles Scribner's Sons (*My Early Life* by Winston S. Churchill); Odhams Books Ltd (*London to Ladysmith Via Pretoria* by Winston S. Churchill, included in *Frontiers and Wars* published by Eyre & Spottiswoode Ltd); Odhams Books Ltd and Eyre & Spottiswoode Ltd (*The River War* by Winston S. Churchill); Hamish Hamilton Ltd and Harper & Row, Publishers, Incorporated (*Inside Africa* by John Gunther); Anglo American Corporation of South Africa, Ltd.

Acknowledgements are also due to *Queen* and to the High Commission of the United Republic of Tanganyika and Zanzibar for permission to reproduce photographs in which they hold the copyright.

To
MY WIFE

To those new states whom we welcome to the ranks of the free, we pledge our word that one form of colonial control shall not have passed away merely to be replaced by a far more iron tyranny. We shall not always expect to find them supporting our view. But we shall always hope to find them strongly supporting their own freedom. . . .

To those people in the huts and villages of half the globe struggling to break the bonds of mass misery, we pledge our best efforts to help them help themselves, for whatever period is required—not because the Communists may be doing it, not because we seek their votes, but because it is right. . . .

PRESIDENT JOHN F. KENNEDY

Inaugural Address, 20 January 1961

CONTENTS

ILLUSTRATIONS

Unless stated otherwise all photographs are by the author and Arnold von Bohlen

Illustrations

PREFACE

AFRICA IN THE span of a man's lifetime has advanced hundreds, if not thousands of years. I am not the first member of my family to record Africa's rise to a position of importance in the world. At each of the three stages in the history of modern Africa—the European conquest, the continent's economic development and the African liberation—there was a member of my family at hand to write about it.

In 1891 while the European conquest of Africa was still in full swing, my great-grandfather Lord Randolph Churchill made an expedition to southern Africa. He arrived in Salisbury, the present-day capital of Southern Rhodesia, only six months after it was founded and in his book *Men, Mines and Animals in South Africa* he tells of the pioneers who came in search of gold to conquer and settle the land.

By the time my grandfather Winston Churchill visited East Africa in 1906 the conquest of the continent was complete: what interested him was Africa's economic development which was just getting into its stride. In *My African Journey* he throws up endless ideas for importing new crops from abroad, for improving the quality of the country's livestock and for extending the recently established railway systems. One project—'What fun to make the Nile begin its journey by diving through a turbine'— was not realized until 30 April 1954 when the Owen Falls hydro-electric scheme was opened by Queen Elizabeth II.

The opening up and development—or the conquest and exploitation (depending on one's point of view)—of the African continent was a by-product of European nationalism. Its result has been to spark off what is perhaps the greatest revolution—at once economic, social and political—that the world has ever seen. It has lit the flame of African nationalism that is now sweeping the continent from shore to shore and even having far-reaching effects across the Atlantic Ocean, as evidenced by the Civil Rights battle that is being fought in the United States at the moment.

While it is impossible to visit Africa today and ignore the cloud of politics that overshadows the continent, this book does not purport to be an authoritative work on African politics. It is primarily an account of the adventures of two young men—with less than 250 hours flying experience between them—who set off on a 20,000-mile flight around Africa in a single-engine aircraft. My book is based on a diary I kept of the journey and I trust the reader will appreciate that the impressions of Africa recorded here were formed as a result of a flying visit.

The many friends—and strangers—who offered the two of us help or hospitality in the forty or more countries that we visited are too numerous to record. But I extend to them on behalf of us both my sincerest thanks for their kindness.

London, 15 July 1964

FIRST JOURNEY

I

AIRBORNE!

It was a cold, drizzly November day. A sharp bite in the north-east wind that swept gustily across Gatwick Airport gave warning of the onset of winter. The airport was almost deserted as a blue and white Piper Comanche lifted off the wet concrete runway, retracted its undercarriage and climbed away towards the low deck of clouds that hung greyly overhead. The small aircraft then turned south and was soon lost to sight.

We headed out over the English Channel with its white-streaked waves, cold and uninviting, 800 ft beneath us. As the grey cliffs of Dover merged with the mist behind us a warm thrill of anticipation ran through us both. At last we were on our way: Africa, a continent of deserts and jungles, a land of excitement and mystery, lay before us.

In mid-Channel we encountered a few heavy showers but the north coast of France was clear. Further inland, however, the clouds lay close to the ground and the already poor visibility was rapidly deteriorating with the premature approach of dusk. We therefore decided to land and spend the night at Deauville. Before touching down I tried to contact Deauville control-tower by radio, but there was no reply. When I repeated the call a second time, it was answered not by Deauville, but by my flying instructor Flying Officer Jeremy Busby (ex-R.A.F.) who happened to be in another aircraft nearly 200 miles away overhead Oxford Airport, which has the same radio frequency as Deauville. He wished us luck on our journey—scarcely one year before he had given me my first flying lesson.

For my twenty-first birthday in October 1961 my step-father had offered to pay for a course of flying lessons for me. At the time the only flying I had ever done had been in the passenger-seat of a commercial airliner which I found tedious. Nor was I particularly keen on the idea of learning to fly myself. However shortly after my return to Oxford for my final year at the University I happened to pass Oxford Airport and thought I might as well find out about it. Seated behind a desk in one of the airport buildings I found a wiry young fellow who sported a red, bushy and unmistakably R.A.F. moustache. His reply to my enquiries was suitably direct—within five minutes I was in the air having my first lesson. Flying a light aircraft for the first time is like handling a small sailing dinghy after having only been to sea as a passenger in the *Queen Mary*. It is something totally different and incomparably more exhilarating. It did not take me long to get the flying bug. Thirty flying-hours is all that is required to qualify for an English private pilot's licence. And putting in an hour a day when I could, I was able to pass my flying-test and obtain my licence by early November.

I have always enjoyed planning expeditions to distant lands; the fact that few of them ever materialized mattered little. I would spend long hours poring over maps, selecting routes and measuring distances. Ideas of sailing round the world, of visiting

Oxford Airport: author and von Bohlen

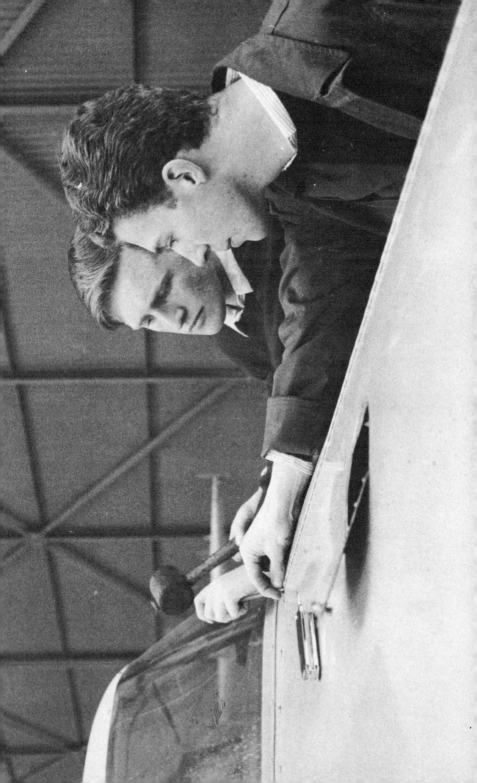

the Antarctic and of making a journey on horse-back following the ancient Inca highways through South America were at various times considered, only to be rejected or shelved. One project however did come off and in March 1961 I joined an expedition to the Tibesti Mountains, deep in the heart of the Sahara. Organized by an American diplomat called, appropriately enough, Livingstone Pomeroy, the expedition consisted of an officer and six men of the Royal Scots regiment, four Americans and myself. Setting out from Benghazi on Libya's Mediterranean coast with five Land Rovers, we travelled some 5,000 miles to the Tibesti Mountains and back across the scorching sands and rocky wastes of the Sahara.

It is difficult to get an idea of the vastness of the African continent. The Sahara alone could accommodate the United States of America; while the whole of Africa could contain besides the United States: Europe, India, New Zealand and Japan, with room to spare for lesser countries. Africa forms nearly one-quarter of the land mass of the globe and is estimated to contain over 250 million people. It is a continent of endless variety and vivid contrast: a land of scorching sands and steaming rain-forests, of hot savannahs and cool fertile uplands.

In the course of my Sahara expeditions I had glimpsed only a small part of Africa and I was anxious to return and see more. The prospect of making a more extensive journey had seemed remote. But once I had my pilot's licence, a whole new dimension was opened up and my horizons were broadened, for a light aircraft would provide a unique means of seeing this fascinating and spectacular continent.

I first met Arnold von Bohlen, nephew of the German industrialist Alfried Krupp, in 1959 in the Austrian Arlberg where we were both skiing for Oxford University. And for three successive winters the two of us ran the Oxford side of an

Piper Comanche G-APUZ

organization of obscure origin known as the Oxford, Cambridge and Trinity College, Dublin, Ski Club which annually took upwards of five hundred people from the universities for a fortnight's skiing holiday on the Continent. Arnold who was a year older than me was at Balliol: I was at Christ Church. During the time we were at Oxford together we became firm friends.

In the same year that I had made the Land Rover expedition to the Tibesti Mountains, Arnold had gone on safari in Tanganyika. And he, like myself, was keen to return to Africa. In March 1962 the two of us went to Austria for a week's spring skiing with a small group of friends and one day as we were being carried up a snow-covered mountainside on a chair-lift, our conversation turned to Africa. We were both pilots. Arnold had been flying for three years and had eighty hours experience: I had been flying six months and had little over sixty hours. By the time we reached the top of the mountain we had resolved to set out on a flying safari around Africa the following autumn. Our plan was to fly out via the Middle East, the Nile and East Africa to Cape Town, and to return to England by way of the West Coast. The advantages of a light aircraft for an expedition of this sort were overwhelming. In many parts of Africa internal communications are virtually non-existent; and despite the fact that most African countries are today independent, their links of commerce and communication are primarily with Europe rather than with each other.

Flying our own aircraft, we would not have to organize our journey to suit the convenience of airline schedules. Nor would we be confined to the cities of Africa which are predominantly either Arab, Indian or European in character. With our own means of transport we would be free to go when and where we chose. It would be up to us whether we surveyed Africa's boundless and varied landscapes from an altitude of 10 ft or 10,000 ft.

The success of our expedition would depend to a great extent on careful planning and on such knowledge of navigation, instrument flying and meteorology as could be gained before our departure. After getting my degree at Oxford in June 1962 I went to spend the summer in America and while I was there I did a course with a company called Flight Safety at New York's La Guardia Airport. Six weeks at this high-powered training establishment went a long way towards making up for my lack of experience as a pilot. During that time I did nearly forty hours of simulated instrument flying and I was able to discuss my proposed flight with the instructors there who provided me with a great deal of information as well as much sound advice. I went into all the different methods of navigation from the old-fashioned sextant and drift-meter, to more modern devices such as Decca and Loran; but most of these aids proved to be either unsuitable or too costly. For our flight around Africa we would have to rely primarily on dead reckoning and map-reading. So as to get some practical experience of navigating over barren country I went out to Los Angeles to stay a few days with an old-time pilot called Bud Gurney who used to fly the air mail with Lindbergh in the 1920's and who today flies DC 8 jets between Los Angeles and Honolulu as chief pilot of United Airlines. Together we made a two-day navigational flight across the deserts of Arizona, Utah and Nevada, overflying the Painted Desert, Death Valley and the gaping gorge of the Grand Canyon.

In early October, one month before we were due to take off, I returned to England and set about finding an aircraft. I eventually chose the single-engine Piper Comanche, a strong and reliable four-seater aircraft with a speed of 180 m.p.h. and a range of about 800 miles. There was a Comanche at Oxford Airport where

I had learnt to fly the year before and I was able to rent it at a rate of £7 15s. od. per flying-hour on the understanding that I would be responsible for the fuel, oil and insurance, but not for the maintenance. Surprisingly enough we had no difficulty in obtaining insurance: Lloyds of London were prepared to lay the remarkably favourable odds of 22 to 1 against the aircraft being a complete write-off. The Comanche, which had the registration G-APUZ, was equipped for instrument flying and had a radio-compass as well as a V.H.F. radio. Arnold and I decided to supplement this with a high frequency radio which, with a range of about 500 miles, would enable us to keep in contact most of the time with the major airports of Africa. The aircraft was three years old and nearly due for an engine-change; before take-off we had a brand new 250 h.p. Lycoming engine installed. Since we had only one engine we had to take into account the possibility of its quitting. We therefore got together a comprehensive survival kit. Besides food and water for a week, we took with us everything from matches and a ball of string to morphine tablets and a ·38 Smith & Wesson revolver.

Several people sought to dissuade Arnold and myself from the enterprise. Some told us that it was ridiculous to make a flight over thousands of miles of desert and jungle in a single-engine aircraft. But since our budget could not run to a second engine however reassuring it might be, my stock reply was that with two engines we would be twice as likely to have an engine-failure as with one. Others more pointedly remarked that with our experience (which by now amounted to almost 250 hours between the two of us) we had no business even being allowed to fly across the English Channel let alone make a 20,000-mile flight around Africa. If we had needed any encouragement, this was it. We took it as a challenge.

Our departure was delayed for three days by fog in England

before we were able to cross the Channel to Deauville late in the afternoon of 12 November 1962. The weather over England, Europe and the western Mediterranean was uniformly bad; poor visibility, low cloud and numerous thunder-storms stood in our path to the Levant. Since there was little likelihood of any change for several days, we were forced to abandon our plan of flying out across the Alps. Instead we had to find a route that would take us over low ground and enable us to keep clear of cloud. We therefore flew down the west coast of France as far as Bordeaux, turned eastwards up the Garonne Valley and on to the Mediterranean. After a night-stop at Nice we headed out over the sea to the northern tip of Corsica and from there tracked down the west coast of Italy, dodging the thunder-storms that lay in our way. A report from Rome Radio indicated that the weather over the Apennines was bad and we were obliged to land at Naples. The next day we continued down the coast, crossed the toe of Italy south of the Apennines and set course across the Ionian Sea towards Greece. We landed at Araxos on the Gulf of Corinth and spent the night at the nearby town of Patras. Early the following morning just as the first light of dawn was silhouetting the mountains to the east we got airborne again. The bad weather of Europe was at last behind us and, once past Athens, we were not to see another cloud until we reached the mountains of Ethiopia.

Flying at an altitude of 11,000 ft we had a spectacular view of the innumerable Greek islands dotted on the silver and azure of the Aegean that was spread out beneath us. We passed over the island of Rhodes with its battlements gleaming in the morning sunlight and flew on eastwards to Cyprus where we stopped to refuel and have lunch. Soon after take-off from Nicosia we saw the pink mountains of the Lebanon rising up from the horizon and, exactly one hour later, we touched down at Beirut Airport.

II

LAND OF INTRIGUE

THE LEBANON HAS been described as the 'Switzerland' of the Middle East. It is certainly one of the few countries in that part of the world that enjoys a measure of freedom and political stability and where, as a result, a thriving capitalist system can be seen. Beirut, by attracting large amounts of capital not only as from the oil-rich sheiks of the Persian Gulf but also from European and United States investors, has become the financial Mecca of the Arab world. I was told that in some parts of the city land-values rival those of Manhattan. This booming European-style city shows marked signs of French influence, for after World War I, while Trans-Jordan and Palestine were ruled by Britain, Syria and the Lebanon came under French mandate. The Lebanon became independent in 1946. Nevertheless, French culture left its mark and Beirut boasts numerous *bistros* and *discothèques*, as well as an enormous casino.

The prosperity of the Lebanon is not confined to the capital alone. As we drove up into the mountains behind Beirut on our way to visit the Baalbek ruins we noticed that few of the people we saw by the way, working in the fields or in the villages, were suffering from the extreme poverty that is so often the rule in the Middle and Far East. The temples of Baalbek were built by the Romans between the first and third centuries A.D. on the site of an ancient Phoenician altar. Some of the columns and ornately carved cornices have fallen to the ground and at the time of our visit restoration work was in progress, but much has survived the wear and tear of time and today the ruins still dominate the broad valley in which they stand. Baalbek's six colossal columns of pink sandstone gleaming in the brilliant sunlight under a sky of the deepest blue against the background of the Lebanese mountains are without a doubt one of the great sights of the world.

Not long after our arrival in Beirut, Arnold and I met a jovial Lebanese in his late twenties called Bassam Freiha who was the assistant-editor of *El Anwar* (The Lights), an Arab nationalist newspaper that is staunchly pro-Nasser. He was delighted at the news that had just come through of the desertion to Cairo of Sahl Hamgah, chief of the Jordanian Air Force. But he expressed disappointment that a couple of days before a group of U.S. Air Force F-104 fighter aircraft had been flown out from Germany to make a show of strength over Saudi Arabia—an action evidently designed to warn the Egyptians who had recently begun large-scale military operations in the Yemen, to keep their hands off Saudi Arabia. 'How can Britain and the United States,' he asked, 'support the medieval and feudal monarchies of Saudi Arabia, Jordan and Yemen, rather than the progressive republican government of the United Arab Republic which, under President Nasser, is doing something for the Arab people?'

'And why,' Bassam added, 'does the United States protect

Saudi Arabia—a land where the ruler pockets more than ten per cent of the national income, has Cadillacs by the dozen, women by the hundred, and a fortune in Swiss and other banks sufficient for him to live in luxury for a thousand years, while his people live in the greatest poverty and many of them go hungry?'

Later, as we were on our way by car to dine at one of the many excellent French restaurants that abound in Beirut, Bassam told me that he was on 'the black list' of Jordan and Saudi Arabia and that twice the offices of his newspaper had been bombed. I remarked that if such a thing were ever to occur in Fleet Street it would automatically be assumed to be a publicity stunt arranged by the proprietor to sell more newspapers. But Bassam took the matter much more seriously and produced a loaded automatic pistol from his jacket pocket to prove his point. Just then our car turned a corner and we saw a military road-block immediately ahead. Bassam was quick to conceal the weapon under one of the front seats of the car. At the road-block we were all made to get out at gun-point while two soldiers in battle-kit frisked us for arms before letting us proceed. Bassam explained that nearly a year before in December 1961 the P.P.S. (Syrian Popular Party) had made an abortive *coup d'état* and the trial was now going on of 300 P.P.S. members on charges of treason. To prevent the rescue of the prisoners or another *coup* by the party which had been outlawed by the Lebanese Government, the court-room had been surrounded by tanks and road-blocks had been set up at various points throughout the city. He added that the attempted *coup* had undoubtedly been the work of Britain, although he was unable to produce any evidence or even to suggest a possible motive for Britain's intervention. Britain gets the credit for every sort of thing in this part of the world. Some people are prepared to believe anything and many have no doubt in their mind that

Britain's influence in the Middle East is as great today as it ever was.

The Middle East, perhaps even more than other parts of the world, is a land of intrigue and the next day at the Phoenicia, Beirut's newest luxury hotel, Arnold and I met two half-brothers of King Saud of Saudi Arabia who were busy plotting the overthrow of their brother's régime. Sipping Coca-Cola in a pent-house suite Prince Talal, the elder of the two half-brothers, told Arnold and myself: 'It is disgusting that my brother (King Saud) should pocket £14 million directly and another £12 million indirectly—a total of £26 million a year from a national budget of £180 million.' Talal, a former Minister of Finance in the Saudi Arabian Government, went on to tell us how he and his half-brother Prince Badr, finding themselves unable to put into effect their plans for the reform and modernization of their country, had defected to Cairo in August 1962. There they had lent their support to the 'Arab Liberation Front', an organization established with the political and financial backing of President Nasser to promote revolution in Saudi Arabia. However in October 1962 King Saud, evidently alarmed by the *coup d'état* in the Yemen, made Crown Prince Feisal Prime Minister in his place. Feisal promised a far-reaching programme of reform which included the abolition of the slave-trade and other such new-fangled ideas. When I suggested to Talal that these reforms, if implemented, might take some of the wind out of his sails he agreed but said that he did not believe that the programme would ever be carried out in King Saud's lifetime.

Events have proved Talal wrong. The modernization of Saudi Arabia has at last been getting under way and Prince Feisal has been able to strengthen his position. King Saud has been forced to accept cuts both in his personal power and in the royal family's income which in the 1963–4 budget was slashed to a meagre £14·5 million. A cold-shoulder from Nasser added, perhaps, to the realization that as members of the royal family they were scarcely likely to benefit from a Nasserite *coup* in Saudi Arabia, induced Princes Talal and Badr in early 1964 to 'acknowledge their faults' and return home.

Before leaving Beirut Arnold and I were one afternoon invited to lunch by some wealthy Lebanese bankers. It was a luncheon for twenty-two people with excellent fare served on the finest silver. Outside the house stood an assortment of E-type Jaguars, Mercedes etc.: inside, the conversation was unequivocal in praise of President Nasser. I was struck by this apparent contrast and asked my host if he and the other guests present would not be among the first to suffer if Nasser were to come to power in the Lebanon. 'Ah! Yes,' he retorted, 'but Nasser won't be coming here.' This, I was to find, is the key to Middle East politics. The vast majority of Arabs have an unbounded admiration for Nasser—so long as he does not attempt to run their affairs.

*   *   *

We only made an overnight stop in the Syrian capital of Damascus, but the few hours we had there were rewarding and enabled us to see a *coup d'état* in the making. Soon after our arrival we were received by the Prime Minister Khaled el Azm in his office. His aura was that of a dignified old-time statesman and belied the fact that he had once, in 1955, attempted to come to power on the Communist ticket. In September 1962, little more than two months before our arrival, he had succeeded in gaining the Premiership with the backing of the bourgeoisie. The Prime Minister, saying that he believed in peace between nations, asked: 'What did you English gain by fighting two World Wars?' I replied that we had not fought for gain but for our freedom which we had successfully defended—this had benefited the whole world. He refused to be drawn out on Middle East politics; and the little dissertation on the need for world peace to which he confined himself was drowned by a transistor radio that stood on his desk blaring out twist music.

By the time we left the Prime Minister's office the sun had set. Arnold and I were led through the ill-lit back alleys of Damascus by a Syrian to whom we had been given an introduction by friends in the Lebanon. In a dilapidated building to which we were taken we met Salah Bitar who was described to us as 'Leader of the Opposition'. This was by no means an official title, for all opposition is outlawed in Syria. Bitar told of his dislike for the government which had recently closed down the newspaper that he owned and edited, because of its criticism of the Prime Minister whom he called 'an old reactionary'. He said he favoured closer links with the United Arab Republic, but not if this meant Egyptian domination as had been attempted in 1958 and which had proved a failure.

While in the Lebanon we had heard that in the course of 1964 Israel intended to divert the waters of the River Jordan in order to irrigate the Negev desert in the southern part of Israel. Although it is primarily only Jordan that will suffer a loss of water, this is an issue on which the whole Arab world stands united.* The Negev project is expected to provide fertile land sufficient to support an additional one million Israelis and there is a common determination among Arab states to keep a stranglehold on Israel to prevent her growth. When I asked Bitar about this he said that any diversion of the waters by Israel would be regarded as an act of aggression by all Arab countries. He added that in the face

* It was the issue of the diversion of the Jordan waters that prompted the Arab 'Summit Conference' which convened in Cairo on 13 January 1964.

of such provocation no Syrian government could shirk taking action. It was obvious that he was referring to military action, so I asked him if Syria was in a position to stand up to Israel in a military conflict. He was evidently angered by this question even being asked and he answered tartly that the Syrian Army with its new Russian tanks and equipment was second only to that of the United Arab Republic in the Middle East and could easily resist 'any Israeli aggression'. When I enquired how many people belonged to his party, the Ba'ath Socialist party, he replied that he could not say, but with a shrewd smile on his face he hinted that we might soon find out.

On 8 March 1963 within a few months of our visit a *coup d'état* took place that reversed the positions. Salah Bitar became Prime Minister: the Prime Minister we saw was forced to flee and take refuge in the Turkish Embassy which, as it happened, was conveniently located in his own house. He was subsequently arrested with five other members of his government and in June the same year tried for treason. He was convicted only on a lesser charge and in December 1963 he was allowed to go free once more. One month before Salah Bitar's Ba'ath party came to power in Syria, another branch of the party took over in Iraq. There was much talk of uniting the two governments and for a while the Ba'ath party seemed to present a threat to Nasser's concept of an Arab unity centred on Cairo. But on 12 November 1963 Salah Bitar, probably as a result of his failure in the Ba'ath local elections the previous September, was forced to resign in favour of Major-General Amin al Hafez and was demoted to Vice-President of the National Council of the Revolutionary Command.* A week later the Army took control in Iraq and ousted the Ba'ath politicians. With the failure of the attempt by

* It is indicative of the changeable nature of Middle East politics that by 13 May 1964 Bitar was once again Prime Minister.

Nasser to unite Syria with Egypt in 1958, and the more recent failure of the Ba'ath to unite Syria and Iraq, it is clear that in the Middle East, as elsewhere in the world, it is nationalism that is still the dominant force.

As soon as it was light the next morning we went to the Great Mosque of Damascus, an enormous building of great beauty. The towering minarets pointing towards a cloudless sky glinted in the rays of the morning sun and looked for all the world like rockets about to be launched at Cape Kennedy. Inside the mosque the bright sunlight streaming in brought out the vivid colours in the dozens of carpets covering the floor that two men were busy sweeping with brooms made of palm fronds. In the centre of the building stood a large tomb which allegedly contains the body of John the Baptist, indeed a strange habitat for a Christian saint. Until A.D. 705, when the Ommayid Caliph, Walid I, turned it into a mosque, the building had been a Christian church dedicated to St John the Baptist. Not far from the mosque is a small secluded garden where lies the tomb of Saladin, the great Moslem leader of the twelfth century who for so long defied the Crusaders.

The sun was still low in the sky when we took off for Palmyra, a small oasis in the Syrian desert some 150 miles north-east of Damascus. Here stand what are probably the most extensive Roman ruins that remain today outside Rome itself. Magnificent archways and tall colonnades stretching as far as the eye can see, rise up from the sand to testify to the former importance of this small haven in the desert and to the power and grandeur that was Rome. Palmyra flourished in the second and third centuries A.D. and in the year 270, under its ruler Queen Zenobia, it extended its authority as far as the Mediterranean and into Egypt. The threat posed to the Roman Empire by the Palmyrenes was sufficient to provoke the Emperor Aurelian to march deep into the desert with his legions to bring to heel the small city and its troublesome queen.

Palmyra owes its former importance to the fact that it lay on the famed caravan route from the East. It was through here that the wealth of the Indies passed on its way to Europe, for the camel caravans loaded with silks and spices were obliged to stop at this oasis for water. The overland route from the East, apart from being long and slow, was prodigiously costly. Each ruler on the way exacted a toll: the Levantine traders and the Venetian merchants took their cut. It is scarcely surprising that the countries of western Europe were anxious to discover a sea-route to the East so as to cut the middle-men out of this important trade. It was this commercial incentive more than anything else that led to the exploration of the west coast of Africa by the Portuguese in the fifteenth century, to the rounding of the Cape of Good Hope by Bartholomew Diaz in 1488, to the discovery of America by Columbus in 1492 and eventually to the voyage of Vasco da Gama in 1498 when he circumnavigated Africa and reached India. It is interesting to reflect that possibly both the exploration of the African coastline and the discovery of America might have been delayed for years, if not centuries, had the inhabitants of Palmyra not been so greedy.

Today Palmyra is a village of only a couple of hundred inhabitants. The camel caravans are rare, their place taken by a bus which, with very dark-tinted windows to keep out the glare of the sun, plies the desert-route between Damascus and Baghdad.

*   *   *

It was late in the afternoon when we arrived from Palmyra at Jerusalem Airport on the Jordanian side of the Jordan–Israel border. A strong east wind was whipping up the sand and dust at the airfield. Since there was no hangar in which to shelter the Comanche we tied it down with stakes and ropes, and lashed the control-columns with the front-seat belts to prevent damage to the controls. Then, as the sun was setting we visited some of the many churches of Jerusalem and walked up the Way of the Cross to the ornately decorated Church of the Holy Sepulchre. From there we wandered around the bazaars of the Old City which one can well imagine has changed but little in the last two thousand years.

An Oxford friend of mine, a Jordanian called Farouk Toukan, had been at Jerusalem Airport to meet us and that evening he took us to dine with a group of Jordanian politicians, including an ex-speaker of the Jordanian Lower House, a one-time Minister of Finance, a former ambassador to London and the editor of *Folastin,* Jordan's oldest newspaper. We had dinner at a restaurant run by Mrs Antonius, the widow of George Antonius, author of *The Arab Awakening.* When we had finished eating she came over and joined our table. On learning that we were discussing the vexed problem of Arab unity, she remarked that she was deeply disappointed that so much was said, but so little done to make it a reality; and she expressed the wish that her husband were still alive to write a companion volume to his earlier work entitled *The Arab's Gone to Sleep Again.*

In spite of the fact that all Arabs from Baghdad to Marrakesh share the same religion, the same laws and the same language, the only point on which they are united is in a common hostility to Israel. The conflict between Arab and Jew for what was formerly Palestine and the creation of the state of Israel on 15 May 1948, has left many unresolved problems. The most serious of these is that of the Palestinian refugees who fled before the Zionists in 1948. The 1963 report of the United Nations Relief and Works Agency (UNRWA) showed that there was still a total of

Palmyra ruins

1,210,170 registered refugees of whom half were under eighteen years of age. There are refugee camps in Syria, Lebanon and the Gaza strip, but Jordan with its small population of one and three-quarter million has to bear the brunt. It is significant that the United Arab Republic which, with a population of 26 million, is by far the largest Arab country, has refused to absorb more than a handful of the refugees. The propaganda value of the refugees, as a source of grievance against Israel, is too great for President Nasser even to contemplate a solution of the problem.

The morning after our arrival the Governor of Jerusalem arranged for a Jordanian army major to take us to the Jordan–Israel border. Jerusalem is not only a Holy City for Moslems, Christians and Jews—it has become the Berlin of the Middle East. A twenty-minute drive by car brought us to Beits Safafa, one of the frontier villages. It was quiet and desolate. But this was only a first impression, for we soon saw faces peering at us from behind veiled windows, showing that the village was by no means uninhabited. The Jerusalem 'Wall' at this point is no more than an eight-foot wire-mesh fence, similar to one round a tennis court, surmounted by strands of barbed wire; nevertheless it fulfils the same purpose as its more solid counterpart in Berlin. As we approached, two small boys, one on either side of the fence, stood talking to each other. On seeing us they both fled, for no communication is allowed through the fence which is regularly patrolled by Jordanian and Israeli military units. The Jordanian major told us that shots were not often exchanged nowadays, but he added that in the last few years he had twice been wounded while escorting members of the United Nations Observer Force, which is there to keep the peace. 'Arabs and Jews have lived here side by side in peace for centuries,' said the major. 'Why did Britain and the United States divide Palestine in order to create the state of Israel? And why do Jews who have

Jerusalem: the divided city

for centuries had their homes and livelihood in Europe and America come to Palestine to drive out and expropriate the inhabitants? Our argument is not with the Jews but with the Zionists.'

While admitting that the Arab case was a strong one, we pointed out to the major that the state of Israel was evidently there to stay and that the sooner this is recognized and peace declared, the better for both sides.

In the afternoon we flew to Amman, the Jordanian capital, which was less than half an hour by air from Jerusalem. A few minutes after take-off as we passed abeam the city of Jericho I pushed the nose of the Comanche over into a dive. The altimeter started to unwind rapidly. It soon registered zero altitude and a few seconds later the hands on the dial passed through 1,000 ft *below* sea-level—still we continued to descend. As we levelled out the altimeter was indicating 1,250 ft *below* sea-level and we were flashing over the calm waters of the Dead Sea which lay only a few feet beneath us. We pulled up steeply as we neared the far shore of the lake and gained sufficient altitude to cross the mountains which stood between us and Amman where we touched down soon afterwards.

At the Ragadan Palace in Amman we met King Hussein who rules this small state brought into being by Britain at the end of World War I. He is a small man but one of the bravest in all the Middle East. His problems are many. He has to deal with enemies abroad and traitors at home. Shortly before our arrival the head of the Jordanian Air Force followed by two other pilots in their Hawker Hunter jet fighters had defected to Cairo. The Jordanians jokingly attributed this to the aircraft having faulty compasses supplied by the British. King Hussein goes daily in peril of his life, for Nasser finds him an obstacle to his ambition of securing dominion over the Arab world. Cairo Radio, an instrument of propaganda that might well have aroused the envy of Dr Goebbels, regularly attempts to incite the Palestinian population of Jordan to treachery, alleging that their King is in league with the Jews to prevent their return to their homeland.*

Despite frequent attempts on his life, King Hussein refuses to be intimidated and continues to pursue his own policies both at home and abroad. The development of Jordan's meagre economic resources is going ahead with the implementation of a seven-year plan; and the elections of 26 November 1962 that were being held at the time of our visit were, according to the British Ambassador Sir Roderick Parkes, the freest in all the Middle East. As for foreign policy, the Prime Minister Wasfi Tel (since replaced) told us that while every Arab hoped for unity this could never come about through the domination of 'a demagogue like Nasser'; for this reason Jordan would resist his expansionist programme as far as she was able. The Jordanian Government was very disturbed by the Egyptian military adventure in the Yemen, believing that it might become a base from which Nasser could subvert the governments of Jordan and Saudi Arabia, and thereby get his hands on the oil of the Persian Gulf. But Jordan was in no position to take a stand against the large Russian-equipped Egyptian army that was trying to gain control in the Yemen and was forced to confine herself largely to verbal protest.

On take-off from Amman we headed south to the Gulf of Aquaba to avoid overflying Israeli territory. We then turned west towards Cairo. Visibility over the desert was exceptional. Mount Sinai stood out on the horizon about eighty miles to the south and we were able to survey the barren peninsula where the Jews

---

* Although this was the case at the time of our visit, the situation has altered somewhat since the Arabs 'Summit Conference' of 13 January 1964. The subsequent *rapprochement* between King Hussein and President Nasser has brought a lull in the propaganda war between Jordan and the U.A.R.

were forced to wander for forty years before being admitted to the Promised Land. As we crossed the Red Sea we saw several large tankers entering the southern end of the Suez Canal; then we were once more over the desert. Shortly before we were due to reach Cairo the desert ended abruptly, giving way to what looked like a dark green sea. It was only after we had checked our maps and gone over our calculations that we realized that it was the Nile delta. Cairo Airport lay dead ahead.

III

THE NILE

Modern Cairo presents an imposing façade to the visitor. Tree-lined avenues, parks and polo grounds catch the eye, while great office-blocks and new apartment buildings command attention. Dominating the scene are the new multi-storey air-conditioned hotels such as the New Shepheard's and the inevitable Nile Hilton which line the river bank.

But first impressions are often deceptive. We were staying with a friend of Arnold's, a young German businessman called Conny von Lüttwitz who lived in the pleasant residential suburb of Cairo known as Ma'adi. An eightpenny train ride from Ma'adi into the centre of Cairo certainly gives one a different picture of the city. It is then that the squalor of the shacks and tumbled-down buildings that line the railway strikes one. Throughout the city beggars, young and old alike, importune the stranger and it is no uncommon sight to see men sleeping in the filth of the pavement in the middle of the day. Behind the western façade presented to the tourist, there is ever-present the grim squalor and misery of the East.

The visitor might well ask what have been the fruits of the rule of the Egyptian military junta and of President Gamal Abdul Nasser in the twelve years since the overthrow of King Farouk. Nasser, by Oriental standards, leads a frugal, even puritanical existence. He has given the Egyptian a sense of pride. He has done away with much of the corruption that existed under the monarchy and has gone a long way towards improving education, establishing heavy industry and modernizing Egypt's administrative machinery. He has confounded those critics who vowed he could never run the Suez Canal efficiently: the Canal has been deepened and is today carrying more traffic than ever before. But in spite of Nasser's social revolution and the large quantities of foreign aid from both East and West that have been poured into the country the lot of the city-dweller and of the 'fellahi' (peasant) has been little improved. This can in part be attributed to a rapid increase in population, but it must largely be due to Nasser's 'Grand Design' which has necessitated enormous expenditure on jet aircraft, tanks and other military equipment bought from the Soviet Union, exceeding by far the requirements of any policy of self-defence. Nasser's military adventure in the Yemen has kept upwards of 25,000 soldiers engaged on foreign soil for nearly two years without any military success whatever. And about a dozen German scientists are currently employed in developing two rockets of a comparatively unsophisticated V2 type which the Egyptians hope to combine into a single two-stage rocket. The rockets are being developed ostensibly for 'meteorological research'; however an interesting feature, as President Nasser himself pointed out in a recent speech, is that they will have sufficient range to cover territory south of Beirut (i.e. Israel). These ventures have been very costly and have undoubtedly placed a severe strain on Egypt's limited resources.

But if Nasser is to blame for pursuing an expensive and

aggressive foreign policy, a large share of the responsibility for it must be borne by those countries that have given aid to Egypt in the past and continue to do so today. It matters little how aid is given. For economic aid in the form of grain makes cash formerly earmarked for the purchase of this essential commodity available for increased military spending. The basic aim of aid, which must be the relief of hardship and the development of a country's economy, is thereby defeated. Nor is Nasser alone in using economic aid in pursuit of an aggressive foreign policy, President Sukarno of Indonesia is another flagrant example. It is time that the Western Powers learned to give assistance that benefits whole peoples, instead of gratifying the egotistical imperialist ambitions of a handful of petty dictators.

If modern Cairo is a disappointment, ancient Cairo comes fully up to expectations. Out by the Pyramids of Giza which stand on the edge of the desert a few miles from the centre of the city, we were able to hire some ponies and ride out into the desert. And in spite of the fact that my pony was under the firm delusion that he was a donkey and could only with difficulty be coaxed into a slow trot, we spent a most enjoyable afternoon. At the foot of the Pyramids there is a thriving trade selling trinkets and souvenirs to gullible tourists, and nearby is the clutter of Sahara City where nightly a lamentable show of marionettes and belly-dancers (now fully clothed on Nasser's instructions) takes place. It is only after riding out some way into the desert that one can escape the turmoil of modern life: the desert is timeless. Looking back across the waste of shimmering mirages towards the Great Pyramid of Cheops that towers above the sand dunes it is possible to capture for a brief moment a sense of the greatness and antiquity of Egypt.

But the most spectacular of all the sights that Cairo has to offer are the contents of Tutankhamen's Tomb which are housed

in the Cairo Museum. These treasures of marvellous workman-
ship and exquisite colour fill several chambers; they comprise,
apart from the personal possessions of the Pharaoh during his
lifetime, everything he might conceivably have required in
after-life, from supplies of food to armies of servants carved in
miniature.

*   *   *

More than 350 miles upstream from Cairo, among the barren
hills near Luxor, lies the Valley of the Kings. The following is an
account of our visit that I recorded in my diary at the time:

> By far the least impressive of all the tombs was that of Tutan-
> khamen. It is small and near the surface. When one considers
> the wealth of treasures that came out of even this small tomb,
> it is impossible to hazard a guess at the wonders and wealth that
> the larger of these magnificent morgues, consisting of numer-
> ous chambers hollowed out of the rock deep in the bowels of
> the earth, must have contained. The extensive and detailed
> paintings on the walls of the burial chambers and passages
> leading to them must have taken innumerable hours—even
> years—of labour by an army of artists working in the hot and
> humid, air-starved rooms with little or no light to illuminate
> their lives' labour which was condemned, so they must have
> supposed, to remain in the deep, dark caverns for eternity,
> unseen by human eye. It is curious to reflect on the power of
> these Pharaohs who were able to keep whole masses of their
> people employed during their life-span on a project solely
> destined to help them on their way to an after-life. Their pre-
> occupation with Death must have been paramount, for as soon
> as they ascended the throne of Egypt, at no matter how tender
> an age, work was set on foot, not to build palaces that might

make their earthly lives more comfortable and pleasant, but in preparation for Death.

After take-off from Luxor Airport where we saw what looked like a large Russian Tupolev jet bomber (NATO code-name 'Badger') shrouded in covers, we headed on up the Nile to Aswan. It is only from the air that one is able to appreciate how vital this river, the longest in the world (4,160 miles), is to the Egyptian people. The Nile is no more than a thin green-brown line of fertility running through a landscape of endless yellow desert that stretches across all North Africa from the Red Sea to the Atlantic. Except where it opens out into the Delta between Cairo and the sea, the greenery ends within two or three miles, and sometimes within as few feet, of the muddy life-giving waters of the great river. If it were to fail for so much as a day, it would mean disaster for the 26 million inhabitants of Egypt. The object behind the vast cost and labour of building the High Dam at Aswan is to prevent any of Egypt's life-blood running to waste in the Mediterranean.

Before leaving Cairo Arnold and I had had an interview with Nasser's personal adviser Mr Hassan Sabry el Khoury. The interview had been requested in Arnold's name and for the first few minutes the Presidential adviser embarked on a tremendous eulogy of Germany and the German people. He then asked us for our visiting cards. Not having one, I put my name and address on the back of one of Arnold's. On seeing the card el Khoury at once recalled the great admiration and affection that he cherished for England. And after these customary Arab courtesies he enquired if there was anything he could do for us while we were in Egypt. When I asked if we could see over the High Dam he appeared delighted and said he would arrange everything.

Hassan Sabry was as good as his word. An Egyptian army

colonel was at Aswan Airport to meet us and he provided us with a guide. We had created a bit of a stir at the airport by inadvertently overflying the old Aswan dam which had two manned anti-aircraft guns on it. The old dam, which our guide rather shyly confessed had been built by the British shortly after the turn of the century, still stands today; but the old reservoir is a mere duck pond in comparison to the one to be formed by the new High Dam. If all goes according to plan Lake Nasser, as it is to be called, will extend more than three hundred miles upstream swamping Wadi Halfa in the Sudan and will be the biggest man-made lake in the world.

Our guide took us first of all to see a table-sized working-model of the dam which, we had heard in Cairo, had been visited by President Nasser a few weeks before. In honour of the President it had been filled with water—the dam had promptly given way.

Next we went to see the enormous diversion channel on the east side of the river. Here in a great chasm two or three hundred feet deep work was in full swing. The noise was terrific. Dozens of Swedish rock drills were in operation boring holes into the granite which was then blasted out with dynamite. Giant Russian trucks with tyres five feet high were moving away great loads of boulders that had already been blasted loose, at a rate of about three truck-loads a minute. These were being transported to the coffer (foundation) dam which was soon to be completed. Our guide assured us that the main dam would be completed 'on schedule' in 1968—a schedule that has had to be revised from the original one of 1964.

Near the entrance to the diversion channel a group of angry workmen took our guide to task for allowing us to take photographs which they said were forbidden. We had been permitted to photograph very freely except when we had gone underground to see the giant turbine tunnels, each about twice the size of an Underground railway tunnel, through which the waters of the Nile will flow at terrific pressure driving a battery of electrical generators, and here it was too dark anyway. At other parts of the dam the workmen were friendly and were even eager that we take as many photographs as possible. They were clearly very proud of the dam which besides generating 2·1 million kilowatts of electricity will make one million acres of desert cultivable and another three-quarters of a million capable of producing three crops instead of one every year. It is indeed a formidable undertaking the like of which there has been nothing in Egypt since the days of the Pharaohs themselves. Twenty-five thousand Egyptian workmen and more than 1,700 Russian technicians and engineers are engaged in building the High Dam; and the village of Aswan has been transformed into row upon row of multi-storey apartment buildings to accommodate this huge labour-force.

Once the dam is built there still remains the problem of filling Lake Nasser. It is not merely a question of damming the river, for if that were done the banks of the Nile and the Delta would soon turn to desert. During ten months of the year the whole flow of the river is needed for irrigation below Aswan; it is only during the two summer flood months of August and September that there is a surplus that is lost into the sea. Our guide told us that the wastage is estimated at 32 billion cubic metres of water, and it is this amount that would be retained by the dam each year. Allowing for the evaporation of approximately one third of this figure annually, the engineers believe that it will take ten years to fill the lake. But there are many unknown factors to be taken into account.

Further up the Nile the Sudanese tell of a legend that says the Nile will one day alter its course and flow into the Red Sea, and many believe that it will be the High Dam that will do it. An official at the Sudanese Foreign Office whom we met later in

Khartoum said he thought it would take the Egyptians 'at least a hundred years' to fill the lake. Little is known of how much water will be lost through seepage and faults in the vast area of desert to be inundated although presumably the Russian engineers have made test bores to check on this. The most obvious factor however, is that Nasser is not alone in the project of damming the waters of the Nile. Both the Sudan and Ethiopia are busy building their own dams. And Egypt is the last in line to get the water. Even Tanganyika, 2,500 miles from Cairo and well south of the Equator, may soon be getting in on the act. For when we reached Dar es Salaam the then Minister for Home Affairs, Mr Oscar Kambona, told us of a scheme found in the files that remained from the time that Tanganyika was a German colony before 1914. The scheme involved pumping water from Lake Victoria (the source of the White Nile) up to Lake Eyasi, from which the central plains of Tanganyika might be watered. At the moment the Tanganyikans have no money for this project but they are nevertheless actively considering it. Some people believe there might not be enough water to go round and that Lake Nasser will remain a desert. If that were ever to happen the High Dam, like the Pyramids, would be useful only as a tourist attraction.

Having seen both the Valley of the Kings at Luxor and the High Dam at Aswan in one morning, it was time to go to the Cataract Hotel for a late lunch. After lunch we took one of the feluccas that were tied up along the river bank and sailed downstream to Kitchener's Island, an enormous garden containing every sort of tropical shrub and tree. Later as the sun was setting in fiery splendour behind the Aga Khan's mausoleum, perched atop the sand dunes on the west bank, we sailed slowly upstream. I took the helm as the boatman knelt on the bow and turned to pay his evening devotions towards Mecca. It was a peaceful and relaxing moment.

Next morning we went to see an obelisk as large as the one in the Place de la Concorde in Paris, which had been cut out of the granite on only three sides. Work on it seems to have been abandoned because of a flaw that appeared on one side. How the ancient Egyptians ever managed to move these vast slabs of stone weighing several hundred tons it is difficult to conceive. But it is easy to see why the Russian earth-moving equipment which the Egyptians assured us is the largest in the world, is continually breaking down.

We had hoped to be able to visit the much talked of temples of Abu Simbel near the Sudanese border; but the new hydrofoil vessel that speeds up the river from Aswan was not working and we had to be in Ethiopia in time for an interview that had been arranged for us with the Emperor. We therefore said good-bye to Conny von Lüttwitz who had accompanied us from Cairo and who was returning there by commercial airliner later in the day.

*   *   *

From Aswan we followed the course of the Nile to Wadi Halfa. And whereas the day before on the short flight from Luxor to Aswan we had been skimming along the surface of the river often no higher than the mast-tops of the feluccas, this time we climbed to 12,000 ft. Not only was it much cooler at this altitude: it was also safer. This was an important factor since it was the longest flight we had so far made over the desert. After over-flying Wadi Halfa we turned south towards Khartoum across the featureless waste that extends as far as the eye can see. By flying high we were able to see much further and our radios had a greater range; also, in the event of our only engine quitting, we would have more time (approximately ten minutes) to discover what was wrong and to send out a distress signal on the radio before crash-landing. Just in case the worst came to the worst we had taken the precaution of refilling our three two-gallon plastic jerricans with water. We had also supplemented the R.A.F. survival kits we had been loaned before leaving England with a packed lunch from the Cataract Hotel which we determined not to eat until Khartoum came in sight.

As it was, the flight could not have been more straight-forward. The radio-compass functioned perfectly, the needle swinging round to point to each successive radio-beacon as it was tuned in, giving a clear indication of what direction to steer. And although we were out of touch for the first time on our V.H.F. (Very High Frequency) radio because the distances were too great, the H.F. (High Frequency) radio, with its complicated trailing aerial that we had had installed shortly before leaving Oxford, kept us in touch with the airports at Wadi Halfa and Khartoum throughout the flight.

On landing at Khartoum officials at the airport were shocked to hear that we had followed the airway used by commercial airliners and crossed the desert in a single-engined aircraft. They insisted that we should have followed the course of the Nile which would have added nearly 400 miles to our 600 mile flight from Aswan. Apart from the fact that this would have been beyond our range, we had been told both in Cairo and Aswan by the Egyptians that it was illegal to leave the airway which cut straight across the desert; and we had been very happy to take the shortest distance between two points. Within a few minutes of our arrival at Khartoum Airport Arnold and I met some pilots who were working for an English aerial crop-spraying firm employed by the Sudanese Government in locust-control. Having a couple of spare rooms at their guest-house they kindly offered to put us up for the three nights we were to be in Khartoum.

During our stay in the Sudanese capital I met Abdullah al

Ameen. His great-grandfather had been the Mahdi, the religious leader who had stirred up the revolt of the Dervishes at whose hands General Gordon had perished in 1885. And his grandfather, the Khalifa, had led the Dervishes at the battle of Omdurman against Kitchener who had come with a British and Egyptian force to avenge Gordon's death. Ameen said he was still very angry with Lord Kitchener for having killed so many of his people in the battle.

Arnold and I visited the field of Omdurman where more than sixty-five years before my grandfather Winston Churchill, a twenty-three-year-old subaltern attached to Kitchener's army, had charged with the 21st Lancers in what was to be the last great cavalry battle of history.

Near the River Nile on a barren rock-strewn plain within sight of Khartoum stands a small obelisk, the only evidence that this was ever the scene of a great battle. It is a memorial to the officers and men of the 21st Lancers who lost their lives in the battle. To prevent the possible desecration of the monument by the Sudanese, more than 10,000 of whom were killed in the battle, it has been surrounded by tall iron railings. A mile or so from the monument Jebel Surgham, a hill of rocks and boulders, rises out of the plain, dotted with the occasional scrub-bush. We clambered up the hill, near the top of which our taxi-driver found a bullet which he presented to me. It was unused, looked rather old, and had been made into a dum-dum by boring out its nose— before the days of the Geneva Convention! When I had cleaned it up a bit I saw that it was of British manufacture; and it is quite possible that it was an original from the battle, dropped by one of the soldiers making his way up this hill where some of the hottest fighting took place.

It was from this very spot that Winston Churchill surveyed the scene at dawn on the morning of 2 September 1898. And in

The River War he gives the following vivid account of the charge in which he took part, of 400 Lancers against 2,700 of the enemy:

The trumpet jerked out a shrill note, heard faintly above the trampling of the horses and the noise of the rifles. On the instant all the sixteen troops swung round and locked up into a long galloping line, and the 21st Lancers were committed to their first charge in war. Two hundred and fifty yards away the dark-blue men were firing madly in a thin film of light-blue smoke. Their bullets struck the hard gravel into the air, and the troopers, to shield their faces from the stinging dust, bowed their helmets forward, like the Cuirassiers at Waterloo. The pace was fast and the distance short. Yet, before it was half covered, the whole aspect of the affair changed. A deep crease in the ground—a dry watercourse, a *khor*—appeared where all seemed smooth, level plain; and from it there sprang, with the suddenness of a pantomime effect and a high-pitched yell, a dense white mass of men nearly as long as our front and about twelve deep. A score of horsemen and a dozen bright flags rose as if by magic from the earth. Eager warriors sprang forward to anticipate the shock. The rest stood firm to meet it. The Lancers acknowledged the apparition only by an increase of pace. Each man wanted sufficient momentum to drive through such a solid line. The flank troops, seeing that they had overlapped, curved inwards like the horns of a moon. But the whole event was a matter of seconds. The riflemen, firing bravely to the last, were swept head over heels into the *khor*, and jumping down with them, at full gallop and in closest order, the British squadrons struck the fierce brigade with one long furious shout. The collision was prodigious. Nearly thirty Lancers, men and horses, and at least two hundred Arabs

Aswan: the High Dam

were overthrown. The shock was stunning to both sides, and for perhaps ten wonderful seconds no man heeded his enemy. Terrified horses wedged in the crowd, bruised and shaken men, sprawling in heaps, struggled, dazed and stupid, to their feet, panted, and looked about them. Several fallen Lancers had even time to remount. Meanwhile the impetus of the Cavalry carried them on. As a rider tears through a bullfinch, the officers forced their way through the press; and as an iron rake might be drawn through a heap of shingle, so the regiment followed. They shattered the Dervish array, and, their pace reduced to a walk, scrambled out of the *khor* on the further side, leaving a score of troopers behind them, and dragging on with the charge more than a thousand Arabs. Then, and not until then, the killing began; and thereafter each man saw the world along his lance, under his guard, or through the back-sight of his pistol; and each had his own strange tale to tell. . . . Two hundred yards away the regiment halted, rallied, and faced about, and in less than five minutes were re-formed and ready for a second charge. The men were anxious to cut their way back through their enemies. We were alone together—the cavalry regiment and the Dervish brigade. The ridge hung like a curtain between us and the army. The general battle was forgotten, as it was unseen. This was a private quarrel. The other might have been a massacre; but here the fight was fair, for we too fought with sword and spear. Indeed the advantage of ground and numbers lay with them. All prepared to settle the debate at once and for ever. But some realization of the cost of our wild ride began to come to those who were re-sponsible. Riderless horses galloped across the plain. Men, clinging to their saddles, lurched helplessly about, covered with blood from perhaps a dozen wounds. Horses streaming from tremendous gashes, limped and staggered with their

Final approach to Addis Ababa Airport

riders. In 120 seconds 5 officers, 65 men, and 119 horses out of fewer than 400 had been killed or wounded.

Standing on the crest of Jebel Surgham Arnold and I surveyed the desolate ground around us and tried to visualize how it had looked on the morning of the battle when the plain was a teeming mass of humanity over 80,000 strong (8,200 British and 17,600 Egyptian soldiers against 55,000 Dervishes) arrayed in battle order with their banners streaming out proudly. Five hours later the scene must have looked very different with 25,000 casualties strewn about the field, 10,000 of them corpses, their blood staining even the red rock a darker hue. We stayed there as the sun set, the shadows lengthened and the battlefield was plunged in darkness.

For the visitor journeying up the Nile it is in the Sudan that he leaves the Arab world behind him and first enters Africa proper. Until Khartoum is reached all except the narrow course of the Nile is desert. Thereafter the seemingly limitless Sahara gives way to more fertile lands and one enters upon a great belt of savannah known as the Sudan—not to be confused with the Sudan Republic which forms only a small part of it. The open grasslands of the Sudan stretch across the whole breadth of Africa from the Ethiopian mountains in the east to the Atlantic Ocean in the west. North of this belt lies the Sahara, the land of the Arab: to the south are the dense jungles that are the home of the black African. The Sudan, lying in between, is an area of overlap between two separate cultures and two different peoples; and while the Moslem culture of the Arab is dominant, it seems that the Negro blood of the African has been paramount in determining the features and complexion of the tribes in the savannah belt.

In the Sudan Republic this multi-racial composition has brought unrest and revolt. The negroes in the southern provinces, more than three million strong, resent the domination of the seven million Arabs who live in the north and who control the government in Khartoum. The negro villagers have fled to the bush and terrorist activity against the Arabs, similar to that of the Mau Mau against the Europeans in Kenya, has been on the increase. The Sudanese terrorist organization is called Anya-Nya after a deadly insect found in the area. In the face of this revolt the Sudan Government has had to send large numbers of troops to reinforce the military garrison in the south.

Khartoum stands at the confluence of the Blue and the White Nile. The one has its source at Lake Tana high in the Ethiopian mountains: the other at Lake Victoria nearly 1,500 miles away in Central Africa. At the fork formed by the two branches of the river is an area known as the Gezira (Island) which is irrigated by the Sennar Dam on the Blue Nile. The dam was built by the British who did much to develop this area for the cultivation of grain and cotton, which is the Sudan Republic's principal export. And today, although the Sudan has been independent since 1956, she still receives a great deal of technical assistance from Britain.

While in Khartoum we went to see Mr Mohammed Osman Yassin at the Sudanese Foreign Office and, as always when we interviewed anyone, Arnold took a camera along with him. But we found ourselves out-gunned by Mr Yassin. Not only did he have an official photographer to take *our* picture but on seeing Arnold's camera he insisted on showing us the 'marriage between capitalism and communism' that he had effected—a Russian camera with a West German lens. However after twenty minutes spent trying to put a new film in, he concluded that the 'marriage' was unsatisfactory and that the result was a 'bastard'. Only after this digression were we able to ask him about his country.

Personal bickering among politicians and the political rivalry of the various parties and religious sects had brought the Sudan's experiment in democracy to an end in 1958, only two years after independence. Since then the country has been under the military dictatorship of General Ibrahim Abboud who, by stopping political squabbles at home and refraining from military ventures abroad, has succeeded in bringing a mild prosperity to the Sudan. A few months before our arrival the Sudanese Government embarked on a ten-year development plan that involves the expenditure of £512 million by 1972. The major projects are two dams, one on the Blue Nile at Rosaires, the other near the Ethiopian foothills at Khashm el Girba where the inhabitants of Wadi Halfa are being resettled as their ancient home is to be inundated by the rising waters of Lake Nasser. The Sudanese believe that these two dams between them will provide another three million acres of cultivable land; this compares favourably with the Aswan Dam where the less fortunate Egyptians are hoping to reclaim from desert only half this amount with a project nearly ten times as costly.

The Sudanese are a very grown-up and independent-minded people. And while they are prepared to trade with all nations, they are subservient to none. They demonstrated this in 1961 when the Soviet Union, the largest buyer of Sudanese cotton, brought pressure to bear on the Sudan to allow the transit of arms to the Communist-supported régime of Antoine Gizenga at Stanleyville in the Congo—permission was refused. Rather than join in the brouhaha against the 'imperialists and neo-colonialists' or attempt to rock the international boat along with the more vociferous members of the Afro-Asian group, the Sudanese busy themselves with their own affairs. There is no question of their having a 'chip on their shoulder' and their affection for Britain in spite of the battle of Omdurman and after years of colonial rule is remarkable. As one Sudanese put it to me: 'Now that you British have left, we love you very much.'

IV

LION OF JUDAH

Dark thunder-clouds hung low over the Ethiopian mountains that towered up ahead of us. We had planned a dawn departure from Khartoum, in the hope of reaching the mountains before the heat of the midday sun made a great build-up of cumulus clouds with their attendant thunder-heads and turbulence. As the sun broke the eastern horizon we had been at the end of the runway doing our final checks before take-off. But when we ran the engine up to 2,000 r.p.m. there was a drop of 250 r.p.m. on the starboard magneto. Something was wrong. Arnold and I had agreed before even leaving England that there were quite enough risks involved in the journey that could not be taken into account, such as a sudden change of weather or our engine failing, without ignoring the ones that could be minimized. We therefore taxied back to the Sudan Airways hangar where it was discovered that one of the spark-plug leads was bare and would have to be replaced. The correct lead was not available but the Sudanese mechanics managed to improvise something

that worked and by 11 a.m. we were on our way to Addis
Ababa.

For more than an hour after leaving Khartoum we flew over
flat scrub-desert, keeping the Blue Nile in sight off the right wing-
tip of the aircraft. Then all at once the river was lost to view and
ahead a great barrier of rock rose up sheer from the plain, disappearing into a heavy bank of clouds that surmounted it.
Approaching from the Sudan it is not difficult to see how Ethiopia, a veritable mountain-fortress, has never been conquered or
colonized by a foreign power (except for a brief period following
Mussolini's invasion in 1936).

On reaching the mountains the change of scenery was abrupt.
We were flying at 12,000 ft. One minute we had a sun-scorched
plain of dusty brown thousands of feet below: the next the
mountain-tops seemed to tower above us and all was a mass of
greenery, shade and waterfalls. It was a pleasant change, as we
had flown over little but flat desert since leaving the Lebanon. Not
until we had climbed the Comanche to just over 15,000 ft were
we above the rocky peaks; since we did not carry oxygen this was
as high as we dared go. (Commercial airline pilots in unpressur-
ized aircraft are usually required to wear oxygen masks above
10,000 ft.) At this altitude mathematical calculations to estimate
our position or to compute the amount of fuel remaining were
noticeably harder work. There were no towns, roads or railways
to serve as landmarks by which we could fix our position, only
numerous small rivers and endless mountains which were
indistinguishable one from the other. We were unable to tune
in the radio-compass either to the beacon at Gondar near the
shores of Lake Tana or to the one at Dabra Markos which lay
on our route. (Not until later did we discover that they are
switched on only for scheduled services of Ethiopian Airlines or
by request.)

We therefore had to navigate solely by dead reckoning while frequently altering course to avoid the giant cumulus clouds, near which there was terrific turbulence. A violent bump near one of the clouds nearly threw us out of our seats, prompting us to tighten our safety-belts and steer well clear of the others. We could get no reply from Addis Ababa when we called on the H.F. radio to find out whether or not the radio-beacons were operating properly. Instead the R.A.F. station in Aden on the southern tip of the Saudi Arabian peninsula answered and asked the awkward question: 'Uniform-Zulu (our call-sign) what is your present position?' We were saved from embarrassment in the nick of time by the lead weights falling off the end of the trailing aerial, making the H.F. radio unusable. About 100 miles short of Addis Ababa the needle of our radio-compass swung round to show that at least the beacon there was working and that we were heading in the right direction. Two minutes before we were due to land there was still no sign of the airport; then, as we crossed a mountain-ridge, the ground broke away steeply and beneath us in a valley lay Addis Ababa.

Ethiopia has a longer tradition as an independent nation than any other on the African continent; it is also unique in having been a nominally Christian country since the fourth century. It seems likely that this was the 'Realm of Prester John', the Christian Kingdom with which the medieval monarchies of Europe hoped to join in a grand crusade against Islam, and which the early explorers of Africa were so anxious to reach. The Christian Coptic Church is still a most powerful institution—it owns a large proportion of the land and the extent of its influence in Ethiopia today is medieval. The feudal nobility remains in a position of importance. And the authority of the Emperor, who by legend traces his descent from Menelik, the son of King Solomon and the Queen of Sheba, goes virtually unchallenged.

In these circumstances it might on the face of it appear strange that Addis Ababa should have been chosen as the meeting-place for the African 'Summit Conference' in May 1963 and that His Imperial Majesty Haile Selassie I, Elect of God, Conquering Lion of the Tribe of Judah, King of Kings and Emperor of Ethiopia, should play host to the like of Dr Kwame Nkrumah of Ghana. This would be to underestimate the shrewdness and ability of the Emperor who is one of the most capable and certainly the most experienced of all the rulers in Africa. It is nearly fifty years since Haile Selassie, whose name in Amharic means 'Power of the Trinity', came to power as regent in 1916. He became Emperor in 1930 and during his long reign he has done much to modernize this rugged and unruly land. And today, although in his seventies, the Emperor is as astute, courageous and energetic as ever. He rules the country virtually single-handed: his word is law. His subjects still prostrate themselves before him. We heard that shortly before our arrival in Addis Ababa the first Boeing 720 to be delivered to Ethiopian Airlines had landed at the airport. As the gleaming new jet-liner came to a halt on the tarmac the Ethiopian members of the crew emerged—and got down on all fours before the Emperor.

But despite the gulf that separates him from his people, Haile Selassie takes an active interest in their problems. When the Emperor travels about the country by car and sees a subject wishing to present a petition, he orders the driver to stop. The petition is taken in through the window and, if of importance, it is promptly dealt with.

The day after our arrival in Addis Ababa Arnold and I went to the Imperial Palace to request an interview with the Emperor. Near the entrance to the Palace, on the grass verge of the drive-way, lay a full-grown lion chained to a tree. As we walked by the lion stretched itself, got to its feet and wandered lazily over to sniff us, dragging its long chain behind it. Arnold generously offered to take a photograph of me patting the lion on the nose; an invitation which I declined. (This as it turned out was a prudent decision, for not long after we were there a member of a B.B.C. television unit reportedly lost the seat of his pants to the same animal.) At the Palace we saw the press officer who told us that the Emperor had gone to his country residence for the weekend but that he would receive us at 9.15 on the Monday morning.

Addis Ababa, which literally means 'New Flower', stands in a great open valley at more than 8,000 ft above sea-level. And although it is within ten degrees of the Equator the air is crisp and cool. We were staying with the Dutch ambassador, Mr Welsing and his wife, who were friends of Arnold's. From their house just outside the town there was a magnificent view across acres of pine forest that stretched as far as the mountains that walled in the valley. The freshness and clarity of the landscape were more reminiscent of the Alps than of tropical Africa.

Besides being the capital, Addis Ababa is the centre of commerce for a large area of the country and boasts an extensive market. Here we had a marvellous time engaging in marathon bargaining sessions for things we had no great need of such as spears, knives, icons, parchment paintings, drums, silver ornaments and bracelets made of Maria Theresa silver coins which are still in circulation in this part of the world. We soon learnt that it was wise to offer considerably less than half the sum asked for any of the goods. When the bargaining became too lengthy we moved on to the next stall: then the price would come tumbling down. By this means we soon found ourselves laden with every sort of object. At the stalls where grain and spices were sold Arnold got into trouble with a citizen who became enraged at his taking photographs. The man, who threatened to call the police, said that this was a squalid part of town that was not typical of Ethiopia and therefore should not be photographed by foreigners. Fortunately a young Ethiopian medical student who had attached himself to us in the market and had offered to act as our guide took our aggressor to task and saw him off.

Apart from this incident both Arnold and I were impressed by the friendliness of these proud mountain-people whose poverty is terrible. As we walked back to the centre of town we found that a smile to a passer-by was always reciprocated, especially by the young children who despite their dirty tattered clothes were extraordinarily good-looking. Not in the least shy of strangers, they would look one straight in the eye.

The next day, Sunday, I recorded in my diary as having been the most enjoyable of the whole trip so far. Mr John Russell the British Ambassador had arranged a riding expedition up the 12,000 ft mountain of En Toto that overlooks Addis Ababa. The party consisted of fourteen people including the Italian Ambassador, the British Consul Mr Peel, and several other friends of the Russells. We met at the foot of the mountain at 10 a.m. and I was given a small dark Ethiopian pony of unbounded energy which insisted on taking even the steepest slopes at a gallop. As we made our way up the side of En Toto the scenery grew more and more spectacular. Halfway up we came to a small church built in the circular Coptic style which was full of simple but gaily coloured paintings depicting Biblical scenes. Once we were above the tree-line we left the path we had been following and found ourselves on open rolling grassland. We rode on up the mountain until we reached a sheltered spot just below the summit where a picnic, or rather a banquet, was prepared. From our 12,000 ft vantage point the great mountains that lay around us appeared only as gentle folds in the ground disappearing into the distance.

In spite of the altitude the sun was warm and we were all in our shirt-sleeves. Our host John Russell was sporting a splendid Western hat and a pair of high-heeled Texas cowboy boots. He had until recently been chief press officer at the Foreign Office in London and he was obviously delighted at his new posting in Ethiopia. With great pride he told us of his private army which, by permission of the Emperor, the British Ambassador is entitled to have. (This dates back to the arrival of the first British Mission in 1897. The army was at first composed of Indian soldiers; but these were replaced in 1941 by Sudanese of the British Army when British forces liberated Ethiopia from Italian domination and restored Haile Selassie, who had been in exile in England, to his throne.) The Ambassador's army now consists of eighteen burly Sudanese soldiers who, on ceremonial occasions, respond smartly to the command: 'Ambassadorial salute—Present Arms.'

After lunch we galloped for miles along the hill-tops. The only people we met was a group of Ethiopian shepherd-boys with their herd of goats. Except for a thin cotton garment they had only a blanket thrown over their shoulders to protect them from the cold that comes with night-fall. The elder boys carried wooden staffs in their hands and one, to the envy of his barefoot companions, wore a shoe many sizes too large for him on his right foot. They were friendly, but at first rather suspicious when we offered them some chocolate, which they had evidently never seen before. After leaving the shepherd-boys we walked the ponies home, arriving at the foot of the mountain as the sun was setting.

At 9.15 on the Monday morning Arnold and I were shown into the Emperor's office in a building adjoining the Palace. It was a long wood-panelled room with a floor covered in finely worked carpets. As we entered, the Emperor got up from his desk at the far end of the room. From the door we both made a bow which the Emperor returned. Following the established protocol we bowed a second time as we shook hands with him. He then sat down on his throne and motioned us to two chairs on his right-hand side. The Emperor, wearing a tan-coloured uniform with a huge number of decorations, sat straight as a ram-rod with his hands clasped before him. His appearance was stern and dignified, but there was a not unfriendly twinkle in his eye.

The interview was conducted in Amharic and English through the Palace press officer who acted as interpreter. For although the Emperor understands English and is fluent in French, he prefers to speak his own language. Arnold and I were left in no doubt as to who runs the country. I asked the Emperor if he was meeting any problems in implementing his recently announced programme of land reform. (A large proportion of the land in Ethiopia belongs to the Church and the nobility.) 'There are no problems,' he replied, 'for in Ethiopia there is enough land for everybody.' He paused, but seeing we expected more, he continued: 'There were of course certain people who did not appreciate the benefits the country will derive from this scheme. But pressure was brought to bear on them—they now fully understand.'

Turning to foreign policy Haile Selassie explained that since Ethiopia had always been independent she was in a position to help those countries that had only recently achieved that status. He denounced the plans for regional unity of the Casablanca and Brazzaville groups of nations, saying that such regionalism was hindering rather than furthering African unity as a whole. And he expressed the hope that the meeting of African heads of state in Addis Ababa in May 1963 would form the basis of Pan-African co-operation in the economic and political development of the continent. (In fact the conference, although it established an

Organization for African Unity, devoted most of its time towards achieving military co-operation with the aim of over-throwing the European governments in southern Africa. And Mr Milton Obote, the Prime Minister of Uganda, offered his country as a training ground for African 'liberation forces'.) The Emperor added a sharp attack on the Somali Republic for being a 'trouble-maker' and hindering the attainment of these ends. (Somalia which borders on Ethiopia has laid claim to the Ogaden and Haud areas of Ethiopia and the Northern Frontier District of Kenya—territories largely inhabited by Somalis.)

When I asked the Emperor whether he preferred foreign aid in the form of technical assistance, on the lines of the United States Peace Corps, or direct financial aid, his eyes lit up and not waiting for the interpreter he broke into English for the first time, exclaiming:

'Cash of course is first class, isn't it?'

The following day we left Addis Ababa and flew to Diredawa in the eastern part of Ethiopia. Here we were able to hire a taxi to take us to the old walled city of Harar, capital of the province in which Haile Selassie had been born in 1892. The road wound up from the hot dusty plain around Diredawa into the mountains where it ran by crystal blue lakes and passed through thick shady evergreen forests. Harar boasts a primary and secondary school, and both were partly staffed by Peace Corps volunteers.

This was our first encounter with the Peace Corps which had been greeted with such ridicule both in the United States and abroad when it was first formed in March 1961 under President Kennedy's brother-in-law Mr Sargent Shriver. Critics suggested that it was an organization of boy-scouts who would travel the world making trouble for the United States wherever they went. But the critics have been proved wrong. The Peace Corps has been a resounding success; this for three reasons. First, it has given technical and educational assistance to the under-developed countries to enable them to help themselves. Second, it gives a better idea of the West and western ideals than does the camera-slung, cigar-chewing tourist who comes and flings his money about. Third, and possibly most important of all since the United States in the earlier part of this century took over from Britain the role of the world's most powerful nation, it will give Americans a first-hand understanding of the world and their responsibility to it. The success and achievement of the Peace Corps in its first three years have been remarkable. By the beginning of 1964 there were over 9,000 volunteers working in forty-seven countries throughout the world. Not one volunteer had been expelled by a host country and all forty-seven countries had asked for more volunteers—and this at a time when nationalist feeling is running high throughout the world and Communists everywhere were doing their best to discredit the Peace Corps in the eyes of the uncommitted nations.

Ethiopia is a good example of the impact of the Peace Corps. In September 1962, only three months before our visit, 278 volunteers, one third of them women, arrived in Ethiopia. Except for two doctors they were all teachers and they increased by more than 50 per cent the number of secondary-school teachers in the country. Mrs Tadesse of the Ethiopian Ministry of Education assured us that none of these volunteers was being used to replace professional teachers, only to supplement them. She added that the Emperor himself was supervising the education programme and had increased government spending in this field in the 1963 budget. The Ethiopian Government itself was contributing over £150,000 towards the maintenance of the volunteers.

In Harar we met a young couple who belonged to the Peace Corps. The husband was teaching in the secondary school:

the wife was giving elementary English lessons at the nearby primary school. They showed Arnold and myself around their small house which was clean and comfortable. The original idea that the volunteers should live in the same conditions as the local people seems to have been abandoned—Washington had not realized just how badly the other half of the world lived. The volunteers are now more sensibly given accommodation roughly equivalent to that of the native secondary-school teachers. The couple took us next to the primary school where we saw several classes of children whose ages varied from five to fifteen. When we entered one of the classes for the smaller children, who were crowded together to fit them into the room, they all stood up and with a grin on their little faces said 'Good Afternoon' to us in English. They then proceeded to sing a song to the tune 'Frère Jacques' in English with great enthusiasm, if not understanding, helped along by the young American girl who was teaching them. Although we only had a brief glimpse of the Peace Corps in Harar it was enough to see the eagerness of the children to learn and the facility with which they were picking up English. But the enthusiasm of the children is matched by that of the volunteers who, since our departure, have enlisted the support of the local people and have completely rebuilt the primary school in Harar. The impact of the Peace Corps on a country such as Ethiopia where it provides one third or more of the country's teachers cannot fail to be significant. It is fortunate that the West thought of this form of aid before the Communists. Even so the West has had a head-start from tne beginning in that the official languages of the new nations of Africa are, with few exceptions, European— usually English and French. Thus only those Africans unable to get a Western education go to the Soviet Union or China; for there they have to learn a new language for which they are unlikely to have further use before being able to continue their education. **Man-to-man** aid in this form is rewarding both to the donors and the recipients, for each can see concrete results; it is not something that corrupt politicians can squander or embezzle but something that benefits the ordinary people of a country directly.

Addis Ababa: Emperor Haile Selassie and author
OVERLEAF: *Emperor's lion cubs*

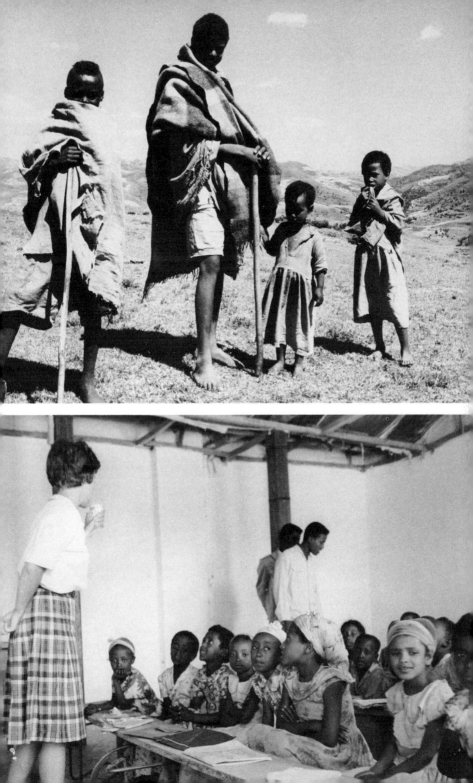

V

BREACH OF THE CHARTER

The purposes of the United Nations are to maintain international peace and security, and to that end: to take effective collective measures for the prevention and removal of threats to the peace, and for the suppression of acts of aggression or other breaches of the peace. . . .

Article 1 of the Charter of the United Nations

IT WAS ALREADY dark when we touched down at the R.A.F. base of Aden, one month to the day since we had left Oxford. The rain and fog of England seemed further away than ever; here the sky was clustered with myriad stars and a warm off-shore breeze stirred the night air.

Our plan had been to head south from Ethiopia into East Africa, but instead we decided to turn northwards and pay a brief visit to the Yemen, the small mountainous country in the southernmost corner of the Saudi Arabian Peninsula. Three months before, on 27 September 1962, a revolution had taken place against the Imam, the traditional ruler of the Yemen, and a

Republican government had taken power with Egyptian military backing. Having only newspaper reports and the opinions of people we had met on our way out through the Middle East to go by, both Arnold and myself inclined to the view that the Imam was a medieval monster who ruled his primitive land with savagery: the Republicans, so we were led to believe, were the powers of Light battling Darkness. Nevertheless we thought we would go and see for ourselves.

Aden, lying at the southern entrance to the Red Sea, is the main refuelling port for ships passing through the Suez Canal. It is also one of Britain's major military bases from which the Persian Gulf oil supplies, so vital to Britain's livelihood, are safe-guarded. In June 1961 when General Kassem, the Iraqi dictator, threatened Kuwait with military aggression, it was from Aden that British troops were promptly airlifted into the oil-rich sheikdom, successfully deterring Kassem from military action and protecting the independence of Kuwait. Shortly before setting out on the expedition I had seen the U.S. Secretary of Defense, Mr Robert McNamara, in Washington. He had pointed out that Britain's military base in Aden was of great importance to the Western Alliance, particularly since the United States had no base at all in this most vital area. And he had stressed that while an increased British commitment to Europe might be desirable, this should on no account be made at the expense of Britain's bases east of Suez.

Two days after our arrival in Aden we learned that one of the three Egyptian-operated Dakotas of Yemen Airlines would be leaving the next morning for Ta'izz in southern Yemen and might possibly go on from there to the Republican-held capital of San'a. But the agent of the Republican government, whom we found in a dingy office in one of the back streets of Aden, warned us not to count on anything since the airline had no fixed schedule.

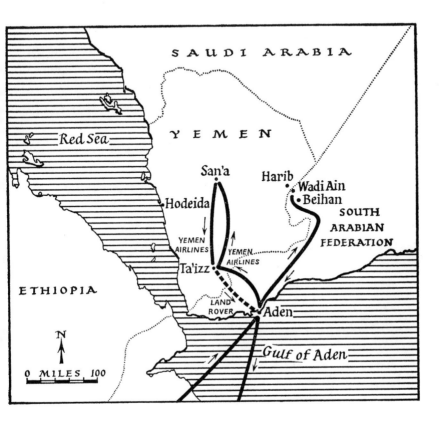

SAUDI ARABIA

Red Sea

YEMEN

San'a

Harib

Wadi Ain
Beihan

SOUTH
ARABIAN
FEDERATION

Hodeida

YEMEN
AIRLINES

YEMEN
AIRLINES

Ta'izz

ETHIOPIA

LAND
ROVER

Aden

N

Gulf of Aden

0 MILES 100

Having received no reply to a cable we had sent to the Republican government requesting permission to land our Comanche in San'a, and having been told by the R.A.F. that even if we did get permission it was more than likely that the Yemeni tribesmen would take pot-shots at us from the 10,000-ft mountain-tops, we abandoned the idea of taking our aircraft and decided to risk taking Yemen Airlines instead.

It was shortly after 6.30 a.m. that Arnold and I boarded the Yemen Airlines Dakota. The aircraft was full of Yemenis returning home with framed photographs of President Nasser, transistor radios and other goodies purchased cheaply in Aden which is a free port with neither duty nor taxes. The freight consisted almost entirely of cases of Vodka and Scotch whisky addressed to the Russian Legation in Ta'izz. The flight to Ta'izz took little over half an hour; but here we were delayed and not even the pilot knew if the flight would continue to San'a or not. While waiting Arnold and I got out of the plane and had a closer look at it. When we saw that several screws were loose and many of the rivets were missing from the airframe we pointed this out to the Egyptian mechanic. He showed no surprise, merely shrugging his shoulders as if to say that he did not have to fly in it so why should he worry. Eventually it was decided that the flight would continue to San'a and everyone climbed aboard. Only after a full load of passengers with their baggage had boarded the Dakota was the main cargo, consisting of a couple of hundred rifles and numerous cases of ammunition, loaded into the rear of the aircraft. It was curious to see that many of the rifles were old ones of British manufacture and had stamped on their butts 'Aden Protectorate Police', from whom they had somehow been spirited away. The airfield at Ta'izz is about 4,000 ft above sea-level; at the end of the one short runway there is a precipice and beyond that, a mountain. As the engines revved up and the aircraft began to lumber down the runway towards the precipice, I said to Arnold that this would be one time we wouldn't make it. But the young Yemeni sitting beside me, who had earlier told me that he was an intellectual and had spent several years studying in Cairo, Moscow and Peking, explained that there was no cause for alarm since the aircraft had been built in Egypt (presumably by the El Douglas Aircraft Corporation). In the event we got off the ground and the aircraft climbed slowly to 10,000 ft. The scenery was dramatic and even at this altitude the mountain-tops, often surmounted by small stone fortresses, towered above us. In spite of being rugged and precipitous, almost every hill-side was terraced for cultivation. In the face of frequent attacks from other tribes, the Yemenis long ago learned to defend themselves by living in the hills and retreating when danger threaten to the craggy mountain fastnesses where it is the aggressor who is at a disadvantage. And still today the Yemeni tribesmen are finding these tactics, developed centuries ago, invaluable even against a well-equipped foreign army, supported by bombers and jet fighters.

The airfield at which we landed near San'a was rudimentary, consisting merely of a gravel landing area and a couple of low buildings, on each of which was mounted a small anti-aircraft gun. At one side of the airfield lay an Ilyushin transport of the Egyptian Air Force which by the looks of things had forgotten to put its wheels down when coming in to land; its propellers were buckled and its fuselage damaged. Several of these Russian aircraft of World War II vintage were based at the nearby military airfield. We learned that they had been converted for bombing and that every morning sorties were being made towards the north-east both to bomb the defenceless civilian population of Royalist villages and to drop supplies to Egyptian ground forces cut off by Royalist tribesmen.

San'a, like Addis Ababa, is set in a valley 8,000 ft above sea-level. But unlike the Ethiopian capital, San'a has a low rainfall; this makes the plain in which it stands arid and the surrounding mountains barren. The streets of the town are narrow and dusty, and the visitor is well advised to walk in the middle of the road to avoid whatever may come out of the drainage-holes in the sides of the houses. One of the most remarkable features of San'a is the size of its buildings many of which, in spite of being made of mud-brick, are more than five storeys high.

The first thing Arnold and I noticed on reaching the centre of the town was a tall building facing on to the central square with its roof and top three floors severely battered. This was the Imam's palace. Three months before, in the night of 27 September 1962, the silence of the dark streets of San'a had been shattered by the sound of vehicles roaring towards the main square. Five or six armoured vehicles, manned by a handful of soldiers of the palace guard and with apparently only seventeen shells between them, had drawn up before the palace and opened fire. The roof of the building had been blown off and the top floors caved in. In the confusion that ensued, al Badr the Imam managed to escape into the hills to the north where the tribesmen were loyal to him. Meanwhile Major Sallal of the palace guard announced the death of the Imam and proclaimed a republic with himself as president. At the same time he sent a message to President Nasser. The promptness of Cairo's response was truly remarkable for this part of the world where everything, except revolutions, takes five times as long as anywhere else. The fact that within three days Egyptian troops were arriving in San'a 'to support the revolution' suggests that even if the *coup* had not actually been planned in Cairo, it came as no surprise to the Egyptian High Command.

Between that time and our arrival in San'a, the Russian-equipped and Russian-trained Egyptian forces in the Yemen had been increased to more than twelve thousand. They held the two main towns of Ta'izz and San'a, as well as the port of Hodeida on the Red Sea; they also controlled the roads between these towns. But in the mountains to the north and east of the Yemen the Imam had rallied the tribesmen who were loyal to him, and although they had only their daggers and some old-fashioned rifles, the Egyptian advance into the mountains was halted. On open ground the Egyptian troops with their tanks, aircraft and modern equipment would have had little trouble in destroying the Yemeni tribesmen—in the mountains the story was different. The Egyptian armour could operate only in the valleys, and bombing was of little effect against the Royalist tribesmen in the hills where the rocks and boulders provided good cover. It was only against the undefended Royalist villages that the bombing attacks of the Egyptians were effective; and here the destruction and misery they inflicted on the ignorant and primitive civilian population was piteous. But it has been proved before that if a country has spirit, the bombing of its civilian population only strengthens its resolve to destroy the invader.

There is no questioning the spirit of the Yemeni tribesmen. They are a hardy mountain people and by tradition a nation of warriors. They do not easily accept domination and even under the Imam, revolts by certain tribes were frequent. But if the tribesmen have little love for the Imam, they have even less for the Egyptians whom they despise as decadent Moslems and a soft, degenerate race of people. And while some of the Yemenis, particularly in the towns, are fighting with the Egyptians, it is evident that a substantial section of the Yemeni population is bitterly hostile to the invaders. The only outside assistance that the Royalists have received has been in the form of money and small-arms from Saudi Arabia across the border. Nasser, in spite of his bombers and modern weapons of war, has had to increase his forces in the Yemen to a figure in excess of 30,000. That the Royalists, without the support of any foreign troops, should have held out since September 1962 against the Republicans and should have denied the Egyptian dictator the satisfaction of so much as one major military victory during that time, is indeed a remarkable feat.

From the Imam's palace Arnold and I made our way to the market-place. There we found a considerable press of people gathered around the small stone stalls which were selling such necessities as grain and goatskins. (The latter are worn as coats for protection against the cold nights.) Craftsmen were busy at work; the blacksmith fashioning daggers on his anvil, the cobbler making shoes on his last. Others sat cross-legged dreamily puffing at their hubble-bubble pipes (which supposedly have a mildly narcotic effect). The tribesmen with their rough bearded faces and turbaned heads, each with a short curved dagger stuffed in the front of his belt, made a vivid scene. Several carried rifles and had great bandoliers of bullets strapped across them; a few even had what looked to be the right size ammunition for their rifles. No Yemeni is considered a man unless he goes armed. The bystanders greeted us with curious smiles and frequently we were asked if we were Russians. When we replied that we were not, they enquired if we were Germans. They seemed very gratified when Arnold admitted to this although they did not quite appreciate his insistence that he was from West Germany. When it was learned that I was British, darkly suspicious glances were cast in my direction. (The Federal German Republic had been one of the first to recognize the Republican government of Major Sallal. Britain however had not done so and has since refused to accord recognition until the Republicans show that they have control of the country, and that, without outside military assistance.)

Suddenly as we were standing in the market-place a great shout went up and everyone rushed off in one direction. We followed. The shouts of the crowd led us to the army barracks on the edge of the town. Here we bumped into our intellectual friend from the plane ride that morning. Dressed in a suit and brown rain-coat, and wearing a pair of dark-glasses, he stood out a mile from the screaming mob of bearded tribesmen who were rushing through the gateway of the barracks. When we asked him what was happening, he explained that a great victory had been won over the enemy and that two truck-loads of captured Royalist tribesmen had just arrived. Stories were current in San'a that the Royalist tribesmen were in the habit of mutilating any Egyptian prisoners that came into their hands, by cutting off such append-ages as noses and ears; it seemed that the Republicans were anxious to get their own back. Our intellectual friend tried to stop us going into the barrack-square, saying that it was forbidden. We pushed on regardless.

A crowd of three or four hundred had gathered around a couple of trucks on one side of the barrack-square. There were piercing yells as a handful of soldiers tried to take the prisoners—a couple of dozen bedraggled tribesmen—from the trucks in which they had arrived to the nearby prison gate. The crowd which was in hot blood began chanting slogans; then there was further clamour and a swirl of dust in the square as some of the onlookers, brandishing their daggers, scaled the prison walls. A smiling Yemeni citizen standing beside me was looking on with obvious relish. Seeing that I was in some doubt as to what was going on, he grinned, then he explained by drawing the finger-tips of one hand from ear to ear underneath his throat.

The sun was setting as we made our way back into San'a along the only tarmac road in the whole of Yemen. The road connects the capital with the port of Hodeida on the Red Sea and was recently built by the Communist Chinese under a technical assistance programme. Except for the odd donkey the only traffic on the road was a few Egyptian military vehicles returning to their main camp which we gathered was situated a few miles out of town but which we were not permitted to visit.

We spent the night at the government guest-house. We had little choice in the matter for there is not one hotel, bar or restaurant in all the Yemen; and San'a must have the unique distinction of being the only capital in the non-Communist world where there is not one Coca-Cola sign to be seen. The guest-house was full of Egyptians and Russians. Arnold and I were shown into a small room with four beds in it, two of which were occupied by a West German telecommunications expert and a fat Egyptian agriculturalist. The sanitation was worse than that of most English pig-sties, and it was evident that the plumbing had not worked since the revolution, if before. The evening meal, served on one long table seating about fifty people, was not very palatable; whether this was due to the thick layer of grease on the soup, or to the fact that earlier we had seen the meat hanging in the open air covered in flies, I do not know. But the red-faced Russian technicians sitting beside us tucked into their dinner heartily. They seemed friendly enough and some even gave us a welcoming nod but since neither Arnold nor I knew any Russian, we had to leave it at that.

The next morning we went to see a representative of the Republican government at the Ministry of Foreign Affairs. 'Why,' he demanded, 'has Britain not recognized President Sallal's government? You British have had correspondents here since the revolution and recently a delegation of Members of Parliament visited us, and still you refuse to recognize us. You British are all liars!'

I said I felt sure Britain would recognize the Republican

government once it had the popular support of the Yemeni people.

'Ninety-nine per cent of the Yemeni people support Sallal,' he asserted.

I asked him why, if that was the case, more than a division of Egyptian troops was required to sustain him in power.

'The Egyptians,' retorted the Yemeni official, 'are here to help us fight the Jordanian and Saudi Arabian reactionaries.'

With this we saw we were wasting our time in San'a and we determined to visit the Royalist side to see what truth there was in this statement, and also in one that had recently been put out by Cairo Radio to the effect that King Hussein of Jordan had raised a regiment of Yemeni Jews in support of the Imam.

It was not until the following day that we were able to get on a plane to Ta'izz; on arrival there we were told that the flight was not going on to Aden except 'maybe after two or three days' (a phrase typifying life in the Middle East). We therefore set about procuring some other means of transport. In the market-place we found a Yemeni with a Land Rover who agreed to collect us at the government guest-house at 6 a.m. the next morning, after we had paid him a deposit of five *reals*. (The *real* or Maria Theresa is a heavy silver coin that soon wears holes in one's pockets. It is the basic currency in the Yemen and its value is approximately six shillings.)

The government guest-house in Ta'izz was a considerable improvement over the one in San'a; it was cleaner and less crowded, although here too there were a large number of Russian technicians in evidence. At the same time there was an American technical assistance group in Ta'izz. But the motives of the two groups were dissimilar. For while the Americans in the Yemen were innocently employed in building a paved road, the Russians, reportedly more than 600 strong, were engaged in the construction of a military airfield.

At 6 a.m. the next morning there was no sign of the driver we had hired to take us to Aden. When we eventually found him in the market-place he said he had been unable to get enough people to make the journey worthwhile and reluctantly returned the deposit we had given him. It did not take us long to find a more enterprising citizen who said we could have the two front seats of the Land Rover for twenty *reals* (£6). To this we agreed and he promptly jumped up on the bonnet of his vehicle and started crying 'A-den, A-den' in a loud voice to the crowd milling around the market. Within half an hour he had found a dozen Yemenis with which to fill the back of the Land Rover and he announced he was ready to leave.

The journey to Aden took more than twelve hours. The narrow road which was unpaved and dusty wound up through spectacular mountain-passes in sharp hair-pin bends with precipices on one side or the other. We stopped a couple of times by the way to take on more passengers and soon we were eighteen on board. During the day we several times met Land Rovers coming the other way laden with Yemenis returning from Aden with newly-bought transistor radios and chanting 'Sallal! Sallal!' as we passed. (It is a measure of the importance of the 'transistor war' being waged by Cairo that a transistor radio is the most prized possession of most Arabs. In Aden we saw people sleeping in the streets at night with no roof over their heads, but clutching in their hands a blaring transistor radio tuned to Cairo.) It was after dark when our Land Rover drew to a halt in a small town. Everybody got out and the driver told us we were in Aden. Luckily we had this time taken the precaution of paying nothing in advance and when we discovered that we were still all of forty miles from Aden we told the driver he would not get so much as one *real* until he took us to our destination. After a lengthy discussion in the course of which Arnold and I, having only a dozen words of Arabic between us, managed to enlist the support of some bystanders, the driver consented to take us to Aden itself.

We reached our hotel in the Arab quarter of Aden after 9 p.m., exhausted and so caked in dust and sand that both Arnold's and my hair which is normally brown, was a dirty yellow. We had a shower and changed; then, feeling much refreshed, we called on Shereef Hussein, the Sheik of Beihan, whose territory the Beihan Protectorate borders on the Royalist-held part of the Yemen. We asked the Sheik how best we could reach Royalist Yemen with our aircraft. He told us that there was an airfield at Wadi Ain within half a mile of the border of eastern Yemen and he said he would arrange for us to be met there the following morning. Delighted with this, we thanked him and made a move to go. However the Sheik insisted that he was going the same way as us and that he give us a ride in his brand new Rolls Royce with which he was tremendously pleased. He seemed a trifle unfamiliar with the vehicle. Instead of putting on the lights he operated the windscreen-washers; then he was unable to find reverse gear. Nevertheless we were soon proceeding at a dignified 25 m.p.h. back towards our hotel. The windows (electrically-operated) were open and the Sheik's head-dress was flowing out behind him in the wind. It was a welcome change after the twelve bumpy hours we had spent in the Land Rover earlier that day.

Next morning we took off for Wadi Ain. Before leaving, the R.A.F. warned us to look out for Egyptian Air Force MiG fighters. Only two weeks before one of them had bombed a village in the Beihan Protectorate and since then a British radar-controlled anti-aircraft battery had been set up in the area. As we would be overflying the battery on our flight to Wadi Ain, the R.A.F. said they would send a signal to warn the battery of our arrival. As it turned out this message was never sent. Unaware of this, and without a care in the world we flew right over the top of the battery, landing a few minutes later at Wadi Ain. As we touched down Captain Oakden of the R.A.F. Regiment, who was attached to a company of Adenese soldiers at the airstrip, rushed across the rough gravel towards us. He greeted us with the comforting news that we had caused a full 'Red Alert' and that every gun in the battery had been trained on us for the last ten minutes.

From Wadi Ain we crossed the border into Royalist-held Yemen where we visited the small village of Harib, where all the houses were made of dried mud. Here we met Abdul Kerim bin Aly who was the Imam's representative in the area. Like several Yemenis we had met he could speak Italian of which we knew enough to carry on a rudimentary conversation. (It is only the Red Sea that divides the Yemen from Eritrea, which was for several years under Italian control and accounts for the fact that some Yemenis speak a modicum of Italian.)

The rumour was current in the Middle East at the time that the United States was prepared to recognize the Republican government of Yemen, provided the Egyptians withdrew their troops. I asked Abdul Kerim bin Aly how this would affect the Royalist position. 'It won't change anything here,' he explained, 'and I doubt very much that Egypt will withdraw her troops— if she did we would win the country back inside a week. But,' he added with a grin as he drew the naked blade of his dagger across the palm of his hand, 'we Yemenis enjoy having the Egyptians here!'

He went on to show us some Russian automatic weapons that had been captured from the Egyptians and he then asked if we would care to see the Egyptians themselves. Followed by a large crowd shouting 'Down with Sallal', 'Down with Nasser', we were taken to a small mud house that had been converted into a prison to accommodate the four Egyptian paratroopers and one infantryman whom they had recently captured. The prisoners, who seemed to have been well treated by their captors, contrary to rumours we had heard in the Republican capital, were all un-wounded except for the infantryman who had a bandage round his head and a very sallow complexion. The Egyptians, we were told, had been led to believe that they would be fighting British, Jordanian and Saudi Arabian troops in the Yemen. But after making an attack on the Royalist town of Sirwa, they had found themselves surrounded by the fierce-looking Yemeni tribesmen who Nasser had told them were to be their allies: they had judged it prudent to surrender.

When I asked Abdul Kerim bin Aly how much of the country was in the control of the Imam, he replied that the mountains in the north and east of the country were all in the hands of the Royalists. He then offered to take us to a Royalist outpost on a mountain near Jehan from which it was possible to see the Republican-held capital of San'a, less than thirty miles away. Because of Egyptian air-attacks it was only possible to travel by night and the journey would take two nights by Land Rover and a third night on camel to reach the hide-out. We were excited by the idea but when he added that Lt-Col. Neil McLean, M.P. reporting for *The Times* had just been in there, we concluded that it would no longer be of news value. We decided it was time to return to Aden and push on south into Africa once more.

We returned to Aden for only as long as was necessary to cable a news-story to United Press International in London reporting on the situation in eastern Yemen. In this article which the London *Daily Express* published the next day (20 December 1962) I asserted that the military position of the Royalists and Egyptians was one of deadlock, which was not likely to be resolved until the Egyptians withdrew their troops from the

Yemen. Writing some eighteen months later, I see no reason to alter this judgement.

Perhaps the closest parallel in modern times to Nasser's invasion of the Yemen was Mussolini's conquest of Ethiopia in 1936. Both these dictators, to avert their peoples' eyes from misery at home and to gratify their own ambition, embarked on an aggressive foreign policy. Both built up a military machine to a level far beyond the requirements of a policy of self-defence. And both, with the overwhelming advantages and the horror of modern weapons, chose to make an unprovoked attack on a primitive and ignorant people; they sought to justify their action to the world by claiming they were bringing civilization to backward lands ruled by medieval tyrants.

In both cases the world organization showed itself incompetent to deal with the situation. There was at least uproar in the League of Nations. Mussolini's action was condemned by fifty votes to one. But in the case of Nasser's invasion of the Yemen, the United Nations ignored the matter for more than six months. Then when the Secretary-General's special representative, Mr Ralph Bunche, was sent to the Yemen to investigate the situation he visited only the Republican side since the U.N. had already pre-judged the situation by a vote in the General Assembly and had decided to recognize the Egyptian-backed Republicans as the true government of Yemen. When eventually a U.N. Observer Force of 200 Canadians and Yugoslavs was sent to the Yemen on 4 July 1963, nine months after the first Egyptian troops had arrived in San'a, their task was primarily to put a check on arms being brought across the border from Saudi Arabia into Royalist Yemen. No effective check was kept on supplies and reinforcements for the Egyptian forces that were being brought across the Red Sea from the United Arab Republic to the Republican-held port of Hodeida and the airport in San'a. Indeed after the arrival

Yemeni cobbler in San'a

of the U.N. Observer Force, Nasser substantially increased his forces in the Yemen.

The United Nations has failed to take action when confronted with a clear-cut case of aggression. It was for this very reason that the League of Nations between the two World Wars proved ineffectual. The League failed to prevent Mussolini's conquest of Ethiopia and was impotent to arrest Hitler's aggressive designs in Europe because the member nations refused to take the necessary steps to curb aggression. Like its predecessor, the United Nations is committed by its Charter to uphold the rule of Law between nations. If it is to achieve this goal it must act with impartiality.

Harib: Egyptian prisoners in Royalist Yemen

VI

UHURU

WE HAD BEEN flying for more than three hours over Somalia's parched grasslands, dotted here and there with stunted thorn trees and tinder-dry bush, when the dark outline of the Indian Ocean came into view and through the heavy heat-haze we were able to make out the white buildings and ordered palm trees of Mogadishu, the Somali capital. As we tried to contact Mogadishu Airport to obtain landing instructions there was a nasty smell of burning followed by a sharp click as a circuit-breaker popped out below the instrument panel. Our V.H.F. radio had burned out. And although we were still in touch on the H.F. radio with Nairobi more than 600 miles away we were unable to talk to Mogadishu Airport almost below us. As we circled the field we were surprised to see a military band drawn up on the tarmac and a large crowd in front of the airport building. The cause of this became apparent when less than two minutes later an aircraft carrying the Somali Prime Minister who was returning from a visit to Washington touched down behind us on the runway.

Livingstone Pomeroy, the American with whom I had made an expedition by Land Rover across the Sahara to the Tibesti Mountains two years before, was at the airport with his wife to meet us. At the time he was working for the U.S. Information Services and he had soon after our trip been transferred from Benghazi, Libya, where we had embarked on the desert adventure. Arnold and I had arrived in Somalia without visas for ourselves or landing permission for the aircraft. This drew agitated protests in Italian from the Somali Police (part of Somalia was formerly an Italian colony) and for several minutes there seemed to be some doubt whether we would be allowed to stay in the country. Eventually a favourable decision was arrived at and shortly afterwards we found ourselves at a reception given by the Chief of Police, a tall, burly Somali with enormous moustachios who was known to all by his nick-name as 'Cosa Fare?' ('What's to be done?').

The next day the Pomeroys with whom we were staying introduced us to Mohamed Seek Gabiu, a member of the Somali legislature, who took us to see the Parliament in session. As we watched the proceedings from the gallery, Gabiu explained that much inconvenience was occasioned by the fact that there was no means of writing the Somali language. So that the debate could be transcribed and understood by all, a simultaneous translation had to be made in Italian, English and Arabic—languages which are in widespread use because of Somalia's close ties with the Arab world and the years of British and Italian rule. At the time of our visit the Minister of Information was having a rough time trying to get his budget estimates for the following year approved. He was being subjected to a voluble attack by a member who demanded to know why, since Somalia was engaged in a grave dispute with Ethiopia over their common border, the Minister spent so much of his allotted budget in transmitting light music to the Ethiopians rather than hard-hitting propaganda. The countries are all too few where government ministers can be subjected to the responsible criticism of the elected representatives of the people and Somalia was one of the few places in Africa where we saw democracy in action. I was surprised to find it working so well, having supposed that an educated, informed and prosperous electorate was a prerequisite of democratic government—requirements that no African electorate can be expected to meet for many years to come. Gabiu explained to me that the secret of its success in his country was that the tribal basis of society had been retained and that none of the tribes would subject themselves to the dictatorship of a man of another tribe.

That evening I dined at the roof-top restaurant of one of Mogadishu's hotels with Mr Abdirazak Hagi Hussein, a young and able member of the Somali Government who had been appointed Acting Prime Minister during the Premier's recent absence in the United States. Arnold had unfortunately been taken ill with a fever and was unable to join us. The minister, who spoke excellent English, began by outlining the justice of Somalia's case in her dispute with Ethiopia and Kenya. He explained that the Ogaden and Haud regions of Ethiopia and part of the Northern Frontier District of Kenya had for centuries been the grazing lands of the Somali nomads, more than half a million of whom today inhabit these areas. He contended that a plebiscite should be held and that these territories should be united with Somalia. A similar scheme for a Greater Somaliland had been proposed in 1946 to the Foreign Ministers of France, the United States and the Soviet Union by Mr Ernest Bevin, the British Foreign Secretary in the post-war Labour government. The project was rejected at that time, however when Somalia became independent in 1960 many of her politicians hoped that Britain would once again support the idea. But the British Government, anxious for the future of the British settlers in Kenya, was in no position to do anything that might offend Kenya's politicians so soon before independence. And just as Dr Shermarke, the Somali Prime Minister, cannot afford to abandon his demand for a Greater Somaliland, so Haile Selassie and Mr Kenyatta could never surrender an inch of what they regard as their homelands without a fight. Thus in spite of efforts by the Sudanese at mediation the situation in the Horn of Africa is likely to remain volatile for some time to come and is ideally suited to the purposes of those who wish to light the flame of intrigue in Africa's explosive atmosphere.

As we were finishing our dinner on the hotel roof-top the conversation changed to the subject of Communism. Hussein turned and pointed over his shoulder: 'You see that building,' he said, 'that's the Soviet Embassy. Once the foundations were laid, the Russians moved in. I suppose they were scared we would install microphones or something. What are they trying to hide anyway?' There is no doubt that the high walls with which the Russians and Chinese surround their embassies and their unwillingness to employ local staff make their motives darkly suspect in the eyes of the uncommitted nations. Hussein added that the Somali Government was deeply concerned about the political indoctrination given to African students in Communist countries. He said that as a result of this all but three of the Somali students sent to study in Peking had been repatriated. These remarks coming from a minister of an uncommitted nation which has links with both China and the Soviet Union were instructive.

In November 1963 the Somali Government announced that it had negotiated an £11 million military aid programme from the Soviet Union and a few days later five Russian cargo ships unloaded a consignment of MiG fighter aircraft at the port of

Mogadishu. Nothing particularly sinister should be read into this event beyond the fact that all arms coming into a continent in such a state of flux as Africa can do nothing to increase its stability. The United States has for several years been supplying Somalia's next door neighbour, Ethiopia, with military aircraft and equipment ($11·7 million worth in 1962). And the fear of displeasing the Ethiopians has prevented the United States from giving similar military aid to the Somali Republic. The likelihood of the present border skirmishes with Ethiopia and Kenya growing to more serious proportions has led the Somalis to turn elsewhere to train and equip their proposed 20,000-man army. It would be a mistake to assume that by seeking arms from the Soviet Union the Somalis are leaning towards Communism: their action is one of militant nationalism and this is the major factor in the politics of Africa today.

*　　　*　　　*

'Uhuru', the Swahili word for 'freedom', was on every lip when we reached Kenya just a few months before independence. For the European on his farm, the Indian in his store and the African in his village, 'Uhuru' was the major topic of discussion. For each it had a different meaning and none could tell exactly what it would bring. This uncertainty gave rise to extravagant hopes and unwarranted fears. There were Africans who saw 'Uhuru' as giving them freedom to take over from the European, his farm, his car and his high standard of living. Equally there were Europeans who believed that an African government would be incapable of maintaining law and order and who were convinced that a Congo crisis would follow hard on the heels of Kenya's independence. Events have proved both these hopes and these fears to be largely illusory.

When Kenya became independent on 12 December 1963 it was an event of deep significance not only for Kenya but for all of Africa where the white man still rules. For Kenya was the first country with a substantial white settler population to gain independence under a black African government. Like India in 1947 and Ghana in 1957, Kenya's attainment of independence marked another step towards the liquidation of the British Empire and the establishment in its place of a Commonwealth of sovereign states. Only twenty-five years ago the very idea of an African government coming to power in Kenya would have been greeted with ridicule, so remote was the prospect. But the world is changing fast and the Englishman of today accepts the principle of Africans ruling Africa with as little question as his father accepted the principle of Europeans ruling Africa. This abrupt change of outlook has come about within the space of a single generation and its cause is to be found in the second of two world wars. Although World War I immeasurably weakened the Great Powers of Europe it still left Western Europe as the centre of world power that it had been for centuries. It was World War II that finally put the old powers in eclipse and brought new ones to the fore. Then for the first time the United States and the Soviet Union stepped forward to play active roles on the stage of world affairs. The effect of this was to destroy the self-confidence and the will to rule of the Colonial Powers while correspondingly strengthening nationalist feeling in the colonial territories of the Far East, Middle East and Africa. A rapid and on occasion precipitate abdication of power ensued, the first manifestation of which came within two years of the end of World War II when India was granted independence after some 300 years of British rule. And it was Britain who ten years later set the ball rolling in Africa by giving Ghana her freedom. Thereafter Kenya's independence was only a matter of time.

The timing of Kenya's independence was judicious. Britain was anxious to avoid a Congo crisis such as had been caused by Belgium's precipitate handing over of power to a government with an inadequately staffed and insufficiently trained administrative organization at its disposal. She equally had no desire to become embroiled in an Algerian War as France had been when she tried to hold on too long. The middle path is a narrow one and with events moving at the pace they are in Africa today there is little margin for error. Mr Harold Macmillan, who made his famous 'Wind of Change' speech to the South African Parliament in 1960, and his lieutenant in the Colonial Office Mr Iain Macleod share the responsibility for bringing Kenya to independence when they did. They also deserve the credit. Britain's major interest was to transfer power peacefully to a responsible African government. This has been accomplished.

* * *

We arrived in Nairobi on Christmas Eve exactly six weeks after leaving England, having flown some 6,500 miles. Arnold had insisted on reaching Kenya by Christmas in spite of the fever he had contracted in Mogadishu. The change of climate was considerable. Mogadishu, lying on the Indian Ocean, was very hot and humid while Nairobi, although little more than one hundred miles from the Equator, was relatively cool, situated as it is more than 5,000 feet above sea-level on the East African plateau. This, coupled with the change in altitude during the four-hour flight, aggravated Arnold's fever and he developed severe earache. On arrival in Nairobi we put up at a hotel and Arnold went to see a doctor who told him that he should go to hospital for the next few days. Neither of us knew anybody in Nairobi but fortunately we had several letters of introduction and the first one we tried turned up trumps. Dick and Daphne Mason had a house and a coffee farm on the outskirts of Nairobi. They told us that it was ridiculous for us to stay in a hotel over Christmas and they insisted that we stay with them. We accepted only too gladly and the turkeys, Christmas puddings and brandy butter soon got Arnold on his feet again.

Kenya is renowned the world over as the land of wild animals. Scattered in profusion on the broad landscapes of the East African plateau they help to make Kenya one of the most beautiful and exciting countries in the world. Until only a few years before, I had been a keen shot and had blasted off at anything and everything. But I had changed my mind. I could find little to admire in the people who came to Kenya merely to climb a tree and, with the aid of an enormously expensive white hunter, line up the cross-hairs of a telescopic sight on some stationary animals and then return laden with trophies to demonstrate their courage and prowess to the folks at home. I had decided to shoot only with my camera except in the case of animals that were pests or were needed for food. Arnold however was keen to do some shooting and as soon as he was well again he arranged to make a weekend safari with the German consul in Nairobi. Instead of accompanying him I went to spend a quiet weekend with some friends in the Rift Valley a couple of hours' drive out of Nairobi. The Rift Valley is part of a fault in the Earth's surface stretching from the Dead Sea as far as Nyasaland; in places it is more than thirty miles wide and is bounded on both sides by steep walls of rock. It has a rainfall in the order of twenty inches a year compared to more than fifty inches in the hills on either side. Because its dry climate makes it suitable only for cattle-raising it has become the home of the Masai tribe: the Kikuyu who are primarily agriculturalists have, like the majority of Europeans, favoured the more fertile uplands.

When we met again in Nairobi after the weekend Arnold, who had returned covered in mud having spent three rather wet days under canvas, announced that his safari had been most successful; he had got an eland, a kongoni and a Grant Gazelle. 'Too bad you don't shoot,' he remarked. I scarcely had the heart to tell him that my 'quiet weekend' had not been so quiet after all. Soon after my arrival at my host's farm a Masai tribesman had come to report that there was a buffalo troubling the womenfolk of his village when they went to draw water from the well and he wanted us to do something about it.

My host and I each took a rifle and went down to the Masai village, a collection of small, round grass-huts. From there, with the Masai as our guide, we made our way on foot through thick bush fifteen or twenty feet high. For half an hour we heard and saw nothing. Then suddenly my host froze. He had heard the shrill cry of the Tick bird that sits on the buffalo's back and warns him of danger. All at once the three dogs we had with us caught wind of the buffalo and rushed into the dense thicket just ahead. There was a terrific bellowing and baying and the whole bush seemed to move in violent tremors. It was only then that we realized that we had taken on more than one beast. We were standing in a small clearing but because the undergrowth was so dense we were unable to see the buffaloes less than ten yards ahead. Had the three of them decided to charge together our situation would have been less than happy since there was not enough open ground to fell them before they were upon us. Fortunately one of the buffaloes, a young bull, attempted an outflanking movement so as to get downwind of us before charging and we were able to drop him dead as he crossed the clearing at full gallop. But there still remained two other monsters in the thicket and because of the effective camouflage afforded them by the heavy foliage it was impossible to get a clear shot and we were forced to fire in the general direction of the commotion in the undergrowth. All the while the dogs were barking, dashing in occasionally to worry their prey and provoking great roars of anger from our as yet unseen adversaries. Eventually we made our way almost on all fours into the bushes. Here we were on ground favourable to the buffaloes. We could see nothing and had no room to manœuvre our rifles. They on the other hand could detect our position by their keen sense of smell and crash down upon us charging like tanks through the undergrowth. After several anxious moments we had managed to edge our way towards their lair. The buffaloes, two large bulls with a good 45 inch spread between their horns, were on the ground but by no means dead; one of them took five shots in the head before we could get near him. One bullet in the right place can drop a buffalo dead, as had been the case with the younger animal we had killed. But once a buffalo is wounded the adrenalin starts coursing in his veins and he becomes almost impervious to bullets. Several Masai attracted by the sound of the shots soon appeared on the scene and rapidly hacked the meat off the carcasses. They returned to their village as dusk was falling delighted with their New Year's dinner.

Arnold and I took off early on New Year's Day from Nairobi for the game reserve at Amboseli where we had arranged for a game warden to meet us with a Land Rover at the small airstrip at 8 a.m. We spent the next four hours driving through the reserve which lies at the foot of Mount Kilimanjaro, and even in this short space of time we were able to see a wonderfully varied selection of wild life—elephant, rhinoceros, antelope, gazelle, wildebeeste, wart-hog, baboon, zebra and giraffe. Some were gathered in herds of fifty or more on the open plain: others stood in solitary splendour among the fever trees. Kenya is one enormous zoo without bars and it is a thrilling experience to see

such a quantity and variety of wild animals in their natural surroundings. Shortly after midday we returned to our aircraft and
set course for Kilifi, a village on the coast between Mombasa
and Malindi. On the way we passed over the Tsavo National
Park and from our vantage point only a few feet above the tree-
tops we had a good view of several large herds of antelope and
elephant. Flying at 180 m.p.h. so close to the ground we had
to keep a sharp look-out lest an old maiden-aunt giraffe poke
her head up to see what all the noise was about. At Kilifi we spent
two days deep-sea fishing in the Indian Ocean from a boat
belonging to Lord Delamere whose father was one of the
founders of Kenya. But although we had a couple of strikes
from barracuda neither of us caught anything. We then flew on
to Mombasa, the chief sea-port of Kenya and the terminal of the
Uganda railway, where we visited the town's bustling dockside
and the ancient Portuguese fort that commands the approach to
the harbour. In the evening we returned to Nairobi.

Nairobi was all excitement. The politicians had just returned to
the capital after the Christmas recess and were preparing for the
elections which were soon to be held to decide which of Kenya's
two major political parties was to form the country's first responsible African government. Independence was expected later in
the year and the political tempo was quickening. During the
week the rival politicians engaged in heated debates in the
legislative assembly and attended to the organization of their
party machines at their Nairobi headquarters. At the weekend
they took off on marathon speech-making tours in the countryside, addressing political rallies in the outlying towns and villages
in an attempt to bring to the mass of their supporters some of the
excited mood of the capital. Only a few days before, Malcolm
MacDonald, Kenya's last British Governor, had arrived in
Nairobi to take up his post. There followed a succession of

garden-parties and cocktail-parties to which Arnold and I were invited and at which we had an opportunity of meeting some of Kenya's politicians. The most noticeable figure at all these functions was Mr Kenyatta. As he stood, fly whisk in hand, surveying the scene with the benign contentment of a grandfather at a children's party, it was difficult to believe that this kindly old gentleman was the same man who had been convicted of managing Mau Mau. One of the guests, a small grey-haired settler, approached Mr Kenyatta and remarked as he extended his hand rather gingerly: 'Things have changed an awful lot since I came to this country fifty years ago.' Kenyatta smiled sympathetically but was unable to restrain a private chuckle. When I asked Dr Kiano, Kenyatta's parliamentary secretary, what he thought of the new governor he replied without hesitation: 'I like him. At least he is more my size than the previous Governors Sir Evelyn Baring and Sir Patrick Renison—they were both such big men!'

Only a few years before, Sir Patrick Renison had described Mr Kenyatta as the 'leader to darkness and death'. Today it is on Kenyatta and his brilliant right-hand man Mr Tom Mboya that the hopes of the Europeans in Kenya are pinned. Should these two men lose control of the situation, the future of the European in Kenya and of Kenya itself would be grim. Unemployment in the country is high and the standard of living is low. The possibility of this well of discontent developing into a powerful left-wing movement cannot be ignored. Kenya has undergone a peaceful political revolution but has not as yet experienced an economic one. A situation in which a small racial minority owns a large proportion of the best land and enjoys a far higher standard of living than the rest of the population creates an intrinsically dangerous situation. Many of Kenya's Africans will undoubtedly soon be asking where are the fruits of Uhuru. If they are not forthcoming, Kenya's present moderate government might find itself ousted by a militant left-wing that would expropriate European farmers as Mr Ben Bella's government in Algeria has done and impose penal taxation that would drive the Europeans out of Kenya. The Europeans' contribution to the Kenya economy is enormous. They grow a large proportion of Kenya's coffee and agricultural exports. They operate much of Kenya's rapidly developing light industries. And although they form less than one hundredth of the population they pay more than 70 per cent of the country's taxes.

Kenya, at this stage of her development, can ill afford to deprive herself of European know-how or to take any action that would discourage foreign investment. The Kenya Government sees this point very clearly. And it is to forestall the formation of a left-wing pressure group that an attempt is being made to tackle the problem at its root and alleviate the causes of discontent by improving the level of employment and by distributing among African farmers land bought from Europeans. Mr Kenyatta, who had so long enjoyed the cordial hatred of the majority of Europeans and who had been the focus of their fears and forebodings for the future, has in the space of only a few months earned their respect and gained their support. When the decision to grant Kenya independence was taken many Europeans complained bitterly that they were being 'sold down the river' by the British Government. Had independence been delayed another five or ten years it does not require much imagination to see that the African political fulcrum would have moved further Left and that anti-European feeling would inevitably have grown, possibly to the point of a renewed outbreak of violence on the lines of the Mau Mau uprising in 1952. It seems unlikely that any party with such a moderate platform as the present Kenya Government would have commended itself to the African electorate had there been much delay. Perhaps even some of Kenya's more stubborn Europeans are coming to see that the action of the British Government may have prevented them selling themselves down the river through their own lack of foresight.

*   *   *

At the opening of the Zanzibar independence conference in London in September 1963 Sheik Muhammed Shamte Hamadi, the Prime Minister, pointed out that Zanzibar was not gaining, but regaining, her independence and he reminded the British that their rule in the island had been no more than a passing one. Only four months later it was possible to pass the same judgement on the Arabs who, with the exception of a period of Portuguese rule in the sixteenth and seventeenth centuries, have dominated Zanzibar with little interruption since it was overrun by an invasion from the Persian Gulf in the eighth century A.D. In 1890 the Arab Sultan of Zanzibar signed a treaty with Britain by which the island became a British Protectorate. Within six weeks of the withdrawal of this protection on 10 December 1963 the Sultan and the ruling Arab minority were ousted by a revolution which had the backing of the island's African population that outnumbered the Arabs by about 5 to 1. Divisions between the Shirazis, the island's original inhabitants who absorbed the early Persian invasions, and the mainland Africans, added to an uneven system of representation gave the Arab-dominated coalition formed by Sheik Ali Muhsin's Zanzibar Nationalist Party the edge over Sheik Abeid Karume's Afro-Shirazi Party which had polled 54 per cent of the votes in the elections held in July 1963. Thus Zanzibar, which had been the scene of racial riots at the time of the 1961 elections when 68 people were killed, became independent under a minority government.

Dar es Salaam: von Bohlen and author with President Nyerere

That Britain allowed Zanzibar to become independent under a minority government might be regarded as irresponsible. But it is doubtful whether there would have been any less bloodshed had the British Government transferred power from the ruling minority before independence. In the tiny state of Rwanda that lies between Tanganyika and the Congo (Leopoldville) the fact that the Bahutu majority took over from their former masters, the Watutsis, well before the country became independent in July 1962 did nothing to prevent the wholesale massacre of Watutsis, some 35,000 of whom are estimated to have been slaughtered in the first few weeks of 1964. An African uprising against Zanzibar's Arab rulers was certainly not discounted by the British Government. It is clear the Commonwealth Secretary, Mr Duncan Sandys, thought it best that Zanzibar should be left to sort out her problems herself and he studiously avoided committing Britain by a defence treaty to the maintenance of the *status quo* on the island. Had he not taken this precaution Britain might have found her relations with the African members of the Commonwealth strained to breaking point.

During the few hours Arnold and I spent in Zanzibar there was little sign of the approaching storm. The palm-studded island with its silver beaches lapped by turquoise waters was languishing in the soporific heat of the tropical sun that beat down from its zenith. The narrow streets were deserted. The heavy iron-studded doors of the houses were closed against the heat. At the English Club overlooking the water-front the island's civil servants were sitting back, a pipe in one hand, a sweating glass of Pimm's in the other. The prosperous Arab merchants were taking their siesta in the coolness of their thick-walled houses. The Africans lay stretched out in the scant shade afforded by the palm-trees. Near the harbour the scent of cloves hung heavy in the air. The dock-hands loading the ocean-going dhows would pause now and then

Kipushi: before taking off into the storm

to gain a few moments respite from the heat by pouring a bucket of tepid sea-water over their heads giving their almost naked bodies the sheen of polished ebony. There was not a cloud in the sky and nothing to suggest that this might be the lull before the storm.

It was only a fifteen-minute flight to Dar es Salaam across the narrow strip of water that separates Zanzibar from the African mainland. Tom Mboya had given me an introduction to his close friend in the Tanganyikan Government Mr Oscar Kambona, who was Minister of the Interior at the time. Newspaper correspondents frequently and confidently assert that Mboya is pro-West. With equal conviction they declare Kambona to be pro-Communist. The use of such epithets in connection with African politicians requires the utmost caution. It is only too easy for non-blacks to view everything that takes place in Africa in terms of the confrontation between East and West. But the Africans have their own problems and while some might be left-wing and others middle-of-the-road they are all basically pro-African. After an hour's talk with Kambona Arnold and I were left in no doubt as to where he stood in the political spectrum. He told us that he would like to see the government party, the Tanganyika African National Union (TANU), become the organ of government. Arnold remarked that if this was his intention he should read the standard work on the subject by somebody called Marx. A fleeting grin crossed Kambona's face and it was evident that he already knew the book well. He went on to condemn the Common Market and to state that Tanganyika should seek aid from the Soviet Union. This was all sound left-wing talk; nevertheless the reasons he gave were essentially African ones. He believed that a strong and authoritarian government was needed to set Tanganyika on its feet. He was against Tanganyika associating herself with the Common Market because he felt that it would be in the

interest of Europe to keep the African nations as primary producing countries just as Britain had tried to do with her American
colonies 200 years ago. He wanted to see his country develop
industries of her own and he complained that foreign capital had
not been flowing in since independence in the way that had been
hoped. He attributed this to the fact that Tanganyika had been
one of the 'good boys' and had so far obtained aid only from the
West. The implication was that a mild flirtation with the Communist bloc would do Tanganyika no harm and might even
encourage West and East to outbid each other in proffering long-
term credits and economic aid. Perhaps he was not so far off the
mark.

Tanganyika's President, Julius Nyerere, is one of the most
outstanding and respected figures in Africa today. He is a man
of noble character and high ideals. Unlike Drs Nkrumah and
Verwoerd he is no racialist. And unlike other popular leaders he
has never sought personal aggrandizement. On hearing of a pro-
posal by the Dar es Salaam City Council in November 1963 to
replace the city's war memorial by a statue of himself, Nyerere
promptly vetoed the project. When Arnold and I went to visit
him at his official residence in Dar es Salaam he greeted us with
a pleasant lack of formality wearing a white beach-shirt buttoned
down the front with bamboo toggles. A slight, slim, soft-spoken
man, he presents a remarkable contrast to Kambona, his number
two, who gives the impression of being solid, determined—perhaps even ruthless. By his own admission Nyerere is 'a school-
teacher by choice—a politician only by accident'. The only pride
he has is for his country. For this reason the Tanganyika Army
mutiny in January 1964 came as a particularly crushing blow to
Nyerere. He felt it as a deep humiliation that within little more
than two years of her proud attainment of independence Tanganyika should have to call in British troops to restore the authority

of her government. The fact that both Kenya and Uganda had to resort to the same expedient sugared the pill only slightly. The way in which the *coup* in Zanzibar was immediately followed by mutinies in three other East African countries brought home to the governments of Africa the intrinsic vulnerability of their positions.

The governments need armed forces to ensure their authority over their people. The problem that then arises is how the governments are to maintain control over the armed forces. For the moment the only solution seems to lie in defence treaties with other states. In January 1964 the governments of East Africa turned to Britain for assistance knowing that she could be relied upon to supply an effective military force which would arrive swiftly and which would depart with equal speed once its job was done. Britain fulfilled the request promptly and efficiently, and she can be counted on to do the same in the case of any other legitimate Commonwealth government that requires help. Nevertheless the governments of Kenya, Uganda and Tanganyika found themselves embarrassed both at home and abroad by the fact that they had to turn to a former colonial power for assistance. And it cannot be doubted that the East African mutinies have encouraged the governments of Africa to make their own arrangements for their defence by the formation of regional and Pan-African defence pacts. These pacts, should they materialize, might form the basis of an East African Federation and perhaps even strengthen the Organization for African Unity to the point where it could assure the stability and prosperity of the whole continent.

VII

LOST OVER THE CONGO

Our arrival in the Congo fortuitously coincided with the final phase of the United Nations' efforts to overthrow President Tshombe and destroy the government of Katanga. For two and a half years the world organization, dedicated by the terms of its charter to the maintenance of Peace and International Justice, had been waging war on Katanga. In July 1960 when the Belgian Congo had become independent the rich mining province of Katanga was one of the few parts of the country where law and order was maintained. In Leopoldville, the capital, Messrs Lumumba and Kasabuvu who headed the Central Government lost control of the situation both in the capital and throughout the land. The army mutinied and ran amok; terror spread far and wide as the Congolese soldiers went on a rampage of murder, rape, arson and plunder. This state of affairs prompted Katanga, which had always favoured a federal rather than a unitary form of government, to make a declaration of independence and to secede from the Congo Republic within ten days of its

formation. Less than a week later U.N. troops were arriving in the
Congo, most of them flown in by U.S.A.F. transport aircraft.
For the next two and a half years and at a cost of over £3 million per month, the United Nations forces remained in the Congo.
But instead of concentrating its efforts on bringing to an end the
chaos and violence that were rife in the Congo, and working to
re-establish an effective administration such as had existed under
the Belgians, the United Nations set about destroying the one
government that had effective control, bringing war and disrup-
tion to the most peaceful and prosperous part of the Congo.

Arnold and I landed the Comanche at the mining town of
Kipushi, twenty miles to the west of Elizabethville, the capital
of Katanga. The Kipushi airstrip lies directly on the border; half
of the rough runway is in Northern Rhodesia, the other half in
Katanga. Less than 500 yards from the end of the runway on the
Katangan side of the border the world's richest copper mine, the
Prince Leopold, stood idle. Power supplies had been cut off and,
without its giant pumps in action, the mine which was sunk one
third of a mile into the ground was rapidly filling with water.
Most of the town's 16,000 population were out of work.

We parked the Comanche to one side of the runway and an
African soldier of the Rhodesian Army patrol on duty at the airfield mounted guard beside it. A jovial bunch of red-faced Irish-
men of the U.N. forces stationed at the nearby frontier-post
looked up from the game of poker they were playing in the shade
of a large tree and waved us on.* They told us that we had little
chance of finding any transport into Elizabethville since petrol
for civilian cars was strictly rationed and there was no public

---

* It has occurred to me that the Irish contingent in the Congo might have
been less eager to help the United Nations put an end to Katanga's secession
had Britain in 1921 called in League of Nations forces to prevent the secession
of Eire from the United Kingdom.

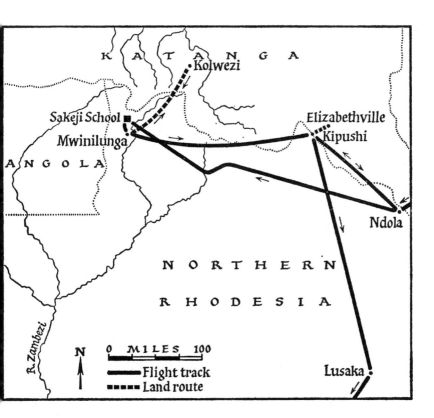

K A T A N G A

• Kolwezi

Sakeji School ■

Mwinilunga

A N G O L A

Elizabethville

Kipushi

Ndola

N O R T H E R N

R H O D E S I A

R. Zambezi

N

0   M I L E S   100

―― Flight track
▄▄▄ Land route

Lusaka •

transport. Nevertheless we set out on the hot and dusty road to the capital. The first cars to come along were driven by Europeans, and our attempts to thumb a lift were vain. But eventually two beaten-up American cars driven by Africans stopped for us. Both vehicles were already well loaded but the drivers insisted that they each had room for one of us. The African who gave me a lift had his three wives and six children with him. I squeezed in behind. With the clutch-plate slipping badly we made our way slowly towards Elizabethville. Several small bridges on the way had been blown up and we had to cross on temporary wooden ones. By the side of the road severed high tension wires still hung limply from the lines of pylons that carried electricity from the Le Marinel dam to Kipushi.

After passing a U.N. check-point manned by Swedes near the giant Lubumbashi copper plant, we found ourselves driving down the broad avenues of Elizabethville, with jacaranda trees lining the fronts of the suburban villas. We were dropped in the centre of the city and to our surprise neither of the drivers would accept any payment, in spite of the fact that petrol was scarce and very expensive. They merely smiled and waved good-bye as they drove off. We then set about finding a room for the night. And although E'ville (as it is familiarly called) boasts more than twenty hotels, the press of journalists was such that it was not until late at night that we found one with two beds to spare.

The next morning, a Sunday, Elizabethville's street-side cafés, with their tables shaded by the gay-coloured umbrellas so typical of many cities in Europe, were buzzing with the news that Tshombe, forever the elusive pimpernel, had once more given the United Nations the slip. He had come to Elizabethville for negotiations with U Thant's representatives, but when it became clear that the United Nations was interested in nothing less than complete surrender by Katanga, Tshombe determined to make a last-

ditch stand at the great mining centre of Kolwezi in south-west
Katanga.

The U.N. headquarters had been set up in the multi-storey
Sabena building near the outskirts of Elizabethville. Here Briga-
dier Raja, the Indian officer in charge of U.N. military operations
in Katanga, told us that within a week Tshombe would be ousted
and Katanga's secession from the Congo ended once and for all.
If Tshombe should refuse to surrender, U.N. forces would attack
Kolwezi in spite of the Katangans' threat to carry out a 'scorched-
earth' policy. Little was happening in Elizabethville, which was
overcrowded with journalists. Arnold and I concluded that
Kolwezi might prove more exciting. The road and rail bridges between Elizabethville and Kolwezi had been dynamited; this was
holding up the U.N. advance until the end of the week. But we
had our aircraft and decided to leave for Kolwezi the next day.

That evening we visited a night-club appropriately called the
'Noir et Blanc' which was packed with Africans and Europeans
gyrating to a hot rhythm. At the bar was a group of young men
in high spirits, whose fair hair and fresh complexion proclaimed
them to be Swedes. They were the same age as Arnold and myself, and we soon found ourselves in conversation. It turned out
that they were U.N. pilots. They told us that their squadron
consisted of ten Swedish Saab J29 jet fighters, of which eight
were armed with 20 mm. cannons and carried eight 150 mm.
rockets each; the other two were equipped for photo-reconnais-
sance. They had recently carried out a rocket attack on Kolwezi
Airport, destroying on the ground two Vampire jets and a Har-
vard training aircraft, the last remnants of Tshombe's small air
force. We told the Swedes of our plan to fly to Kolwezi and asked
them if they would be good enough not to shoot down our small
Comanche which was painted blue and white (the U.N. colours).
They assured us they would not, but expressed doubts that

Tshombe's gendarmes (African soldiers) would extend us the same courtesy if we attempted to land at Kolwezi.

Before leaving for Kolwezi the following morning, we paid a visit on M. Sohier, secretary-general of the Union Minière du Haut Katanga, the great Belgian mining company that virtually runs Katanga. Its fabulously wealthy mines and giant processing plants account for a considerable percentage of the world production of copper (7·5 per cent), radium (90 per cent), cobalt (60 per cent), germanium (16 per cent), manganese (5 per cent), zinc (3·9 per cent), cadmium (3·5 per cent), and silver (1·6 per cent), besides lesser quantities of gold, platinum, uranium, columbium, tantalium, iron and coal. Nor is this the limit to the Union Minière's activities. The company with its associated industries employs a work-force of more than 100,000, and provides houses, schools, hospitals, roads, railways and electricity throughout Katanga.

M. Sohier, a heavy middle-aged Belgian, was seated behind his desk. The lines on his face and the dark bags under his large sorrowful eyes showed the strain under which he had been working. The telephone on his desk rang. He answered it and slumped dejectedly in his chair. He replaced the receiver and told us that only a quarter of an hour before, men armed with sub-machine guns had entered the house of one of the Union Minière's employees, herded the family into the toilet at gun-point and ransacked the house. A couple of days before another employee's wife had been raped. He explained that the United Nations had released the common criminals imprisoned in the two jails in Elizabethville and the one in Jadotville, and since that time crime and violence had been rife in the city. He said he could not understand the policy of the United Nations, nor its justification—it had brought rapine and chaos to the one part of the Congo where there had been law and order. When I asked Sohier if the Union

Minière had been dabbling in politics and giving Tshombe its backing he replied: 'Our interest is to run our business: this means producing copper. We pay a percentage (approximately 40 per cent) of our earnings to the Katangan Government because that is the government in power here at the moment. If the Central Congolese Government were in power, it is to them that we would be paying the royalties. We have no interest in this war—it is losing us 10 million Belgian francs per day (£72,000)—all we want is peace.' Sohier believed that the military defeat of Tshombe by the U.N. would achieve nothing in the long run. 'Who is going to run the country once the Katangan administration is destroyed?' he asked rhetorically. 'Administrators from the Congolese Central Government backed up by the undisciplined A.N.C. (National Congolese Army) will be driven out of Katanga the day the U.N. troops withdraw. The tribes of Katanga will never willingly submit to the rule of people from other tribes a thousand miles away who are unable even to speak their language.'

Like the U.N. pilots the night before, Sohier advised us against flying direct to Kolwezi. He suggested that we fly instead to Mwinilunga, a village in the north-west corner of Northern Rhodesia near the borders of Angola and the Congo. He told us that it was from there that the beleaguered town of Kolwezi was being supplied with food by Union Minière convoys and he thought that we stood a good chance of getting a ride on one of them if we did not mind sitting for several hours on carcasses of frozen meat.

Accepting this advice, we left Elizabethville and set out for Kipushi where we had left our aircraft. We were driven to the airport by two German journalists called Elten and Lebeck whom we had met the day before. Since they had a car and we had an aeroplane we had agreed to pool our resources. They chauffeured us around Elizabethville: we, in return, offered to pilot them to Kolwezi, as we had two spare seats in the Comanche. They had little idea of the dangers they were letting themselves in for.

From Kipushi we were obliged to return to Ndola, one of the Northern Rhodesia Copper Belt towns, to clear customs and re-fuel. Thus it was not until 4.49 p.m. that we got airborne on our way to Mwinilunga which we planned to reach at 6.30 p.m., half an hour before sunset. We had made it a rule never to fly in the afternoon in this part of the world where the heat of the sun and the humidity combine to make a build-up of clouds which late in the day develop into violent thunder-storms. But there was no time to be lost if we were to reach Kolwezi before Tshombe surrendered or the United Nations attacked.

The cumulus clouds of Equatorial Africa are unsurpassed in their majesty. But the gleaming crests which tower serenely to fifty or sixty thousand feet conceal the terrible forces of Nature that have engendered them—forces which have been known to rend a large airliner in pieces and scatter the débris over an area of several square miles.

But over an hour out from Ndola, where in 1961 the aircraft carrying Dag Hammarskjöld, the United Nations Secretary-General, crashed killing all on board, we flew into a violent thunder-storm. We had for a while been dodging the thunder-storms that lay across our path but now the clouds, dark and threatening, closed in on all sides. The crackling in the High Frequency radio due to electrical interference became so intense that I had to remove my ear-phones—I had already lost radio contact with Salisbury Air Traffic Control and had been unable to make my last position report. The radio-compass needle swung round aimlessly, pointing first at one cloud and then another. In a minute we were in torrential rain and had lost sight of the ground. Neither Arnold nor I was qualified to fly on instruments, but fortunately I had taken the precaution of doing about forty hours of simulated instrument flight before setting out for Africa.

We had been flying only a few hundred feet above ground-level when we entered the storm; the first thing to be done was to gain altitude. As we climbed it grew darker. I switched on the panel lighting and kept my eyes fixed on the instruments, so as not to be blinded by the flashes of lightning. Suddenly we ran into severe turbulence which flung the aircraft about violently. The pressure on the two control-columns was terrific and the wings were flexing under the force of successive updraughts and down-draughts. We cut back the power and reduced our speed from 150 to 100 knots to lessen the strain on the aircraft. We pulled our safety-belts as tight as they would go and, with an anxious glance at the wings to make sure they were still there, we headed onwards through the darkness.

After twenty minutes of severe buffeting we emerged from the storm. The sky ahead was clear, but on the vast expanse of horizon that opened up before us there was no landmark to be seen—not a track, not a village, not even an isolated farmhouse by which we could check our position. To make matters worse our U.S. Air Force maps which had proved so good hitherto, had printed across them in this area 'Relief data unreliable'. With neither a landmark in sight nor a radio-beacon for miles around, it was soon apparent that we were *lost*.

When we had first entered the storm our two passengers had jokingly remarked from the back seat: 'This will make a good headline for our magazine—"Churchill and Krupp—lost over the Congo".' As it dawned on them that it was 'Churchill, Krupp and two *Stern* reporters—lost over the Congo', the back-seat humour came to an abrupt end and a silence more appropriate to our predicament took its place.

All the way out from England the flying had been straight-forward. At every stage of the journey so far we had been able to keep in radio contact with at least one major airport. Prominent landmarks and radio bearings had usually enabled us to establish our position accurately at any given moment and in most cases there had been a radio-beacon on which we could home at our destination. It had all been too easy and we had become over-confident. We now realized that in allowing only half an hour before sunset to find Mwinilunga, a small airstrip set in desolate country, we had made a serious—possibly fatal—mistake. But there was no time for such recriminations. We had to devote all our attention to the problem of extricating our passengers and ourselves from imminent catastrophe. Only a few minutes of day-light remained.

While Arnold flew the plane, I set about trying to get an esti-mate of our position by dead reckoning. This was not easy to do with any degree of accuracy because in an attempt to avoid the thunder-clouds we had altered course several times before entering the storm and we had no accurate idea of which way the wind had been blowing us. The alterations of course and the reduction of speed in the storm had cost us valuable minutes of daylight; by my calculations we would reach Mwinilunga at 6.52 p.m.—sunset was at 7.00 p.m.; and, so near the Equator, the light fails fast.

Nothing showed up at 6.52. We strained our eyes in every direction but except for innumerable streams—swollen by the recent cloudburst and glittering in the evening light—nothing interrupted the greenery of bush and jungle that stretched as far as the eye could see across the 5,000 ft plateau that forms the water-shed of Central Africa. We flew on for another five minutes desperately scanning the horizon as the sun sank in the sky. I quickly computed that if the wind against us was no more than 20 knots we could get back to Ndola, the only airfield with night-landing facilities within our range, with fifteen minutes' fuel left. But what if the thunder-storms were still in our path and the wind against us was stronger? (We later discovered it had been 30 knots.) It was by no means certain that we could reach Ndola: and to crash-land after dark would be fatal. We had only three minutes in which to get the Comanche on the ground, then the sun would dip below the horizon and darkness would steal swiftly across the plain. Beneath us the thick bush now and then gave way to more open terrain, but the ground was uneven and water-logged. We knew we would be lucky if it was only the plane that was wrecked in an attempt to make a forced landing in this sort of country.

The sun was just settling on the horizon. The light was failing, and with it our hopes. Suddenly out of the corner of my right eye I caught sight of a faint light-coloured line among some woods about a mile to the north. 'An airfield!' I shouted as I grabbed the control-column and banked the Comanche steeply to the right. It was not until we were actually over it that I could believe my eyes. There, set among some trees, was a short and narrow grass runway. We did a quick run over the field at about 20 ft to check for obstructions. Then we made a tight circle, put the wheels and flaps down, and with our landing-lights on we came in for our approach only just above the stall-speed. Arnold put the Comanche down firmly on the beginning of the runway. At the same instant he grabbed the brake-lever and I raised the flaps (to transfer the load to the main wheels and thereby get added grip). We skidded to a halt on the slippery rain-sodden grass. It was already dark.

As the propeller swung to a stand-still, an audible sigh of relief could be heard from the final exhaust-stroke of the engine as well as from our passengers on the back seat. I flung the door open and jumped out. I was never so glad to have both my feet on the ground. The flash of torches could be seen approaching from some houses hidden among the trees and in no time we were surrounded by a dozen or more people. We were relieved to hear that the voices in the darkness were English. A keen young Lieutenant of the Rhodesian Army, who introduced himself as Roger Bayldon, arrived on the scene at the double. His patrol was encamped nearby and having heard us pass low overhead he had come to investigate. He was under the firm delusion that we were some of Tshombe's mercenaries escaping from Katanga; and it was several minutes before we could persuade him otherwise. Meanwhile a steady barrage of questions was kept up by the bystanders. Who were we? Where had we come from? Where were we going? What were we doing? In the face of this inquisition it was some time before we could get an answer to our question: Where were we?

We eventually learnt that we were at Sakeji Mission School in Northern Rhodesia, just ten miles from the Congo border and less than fifteen from the Angolan border. We had passed within five miles of Mwinilunga, our original destination, without ever seeing it and had landed twenty miles further north at this isolated mission station that did not even feature on our maps.

One of the missionaries, Dr Henry Hoyth, told us that he could give us some dinner and put us all up for the night. We accepted with alacrity and followed him by the light of a lantern to a low building where there were two small white-washed rooms with two beds in each. He then pointed out his house which was nearby and told us that dinner would be ready shortly. Elten and Lebeck joined Arnold and myself in our room. It was only now that we were on the ground that we were able to make a true appraisal of the narrowness of our escape. None of us said a word. After a while Elten reached into his small duffle-bag and

Breaking out of the storm

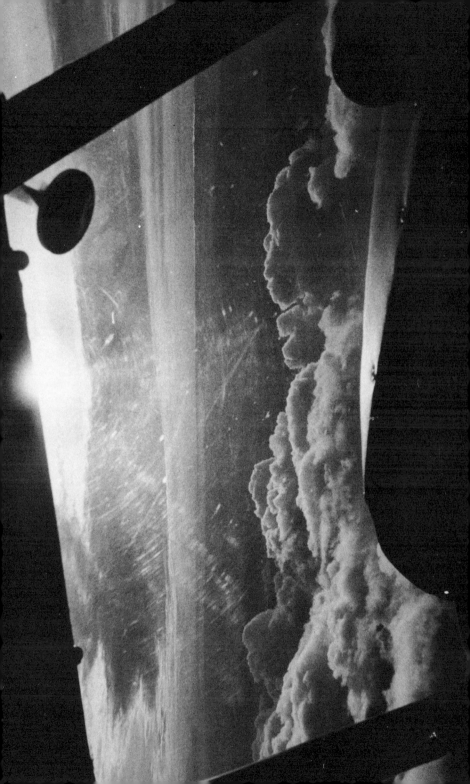

produced half a dozen assorted miniature bottles of brandy, bene-
dictine and whisky, which he had purchased on his flight out
from Europe two days before. Dr Hoyth's opinion of us can
hardly have been high when we arrived at his house for dinner
reeking of these necessary restoratives; nevertheless his daughter
dished up an excellent meal which we all tucked into with gusto.

Dr Hoyth told us over dinner that he had come to Sakeji as
a missionary before World War I and had stayed until 1947 when
he had retired and returned to England. Recently he had come out
again to Rhodesia to be with his daughter who was teaching at the
mission school. He explained that he belonged to the Brethren
Mission and that Sakeji was a school for teaching the children of
missionaries. These children, numbering 116 in all, came from
missions up to 300 miles away in the Congo and Angola. The airstrip had been built not long before as it was only by air that
children could be brought to Sakeji from the more remote areas.
It struck me as rather odd that the missionaries should not educate
their own children in the schools they run for the Africans, but
our host explained that this was the only way that missionaries'
children could get a reasonable education, for that given to the
African children was necessarily more elementary.

After dinner Jim Hess, a tall fair-haired Rhodesian who was the
son of the principal of the school, took us across to the mission's
communal sitting-room where two or three of the womenfolk
were busy knitting. When I asked how they managed to get
electric light in such a remote part of the world, he told me with
pride of the mission's hydro-electric scheme—a small water-wheel
that turned a generator and produced $1\frac{1}{2}$ kilowatts of electricity.
There was always an abundance of water to drive it, for in this
part of the world it rains almost every afternoon and Sakeji School
lies on one of the water-sheds of the African continent. Within
a few miles of the mission rise the head-waters of both the Congo

Sakeji School: before critical take-off

and Zambezi rivers, the one flowing north and west to the Atlantic, the other south and east to the Indian Ocean. After we had heard about the mission and had told our hosts of our journey and of our plan of reaching Kolwezi before the U.N. did, Jim Hess got up and read from the Bible for a minute. After the Lord's Prayer he thanked the Almighty for having guided us safely to Sakeji and asked him to make the runway dry enough for us to take off the next morning.

It was not until the following morning when I saw the airstrip by daylight that I fully appreciated the significance of Jim Hess's concluding prayer. As Arnold and I examined the mud-covered runway, he told us reassuringly: 'Of course we've never had an aircraft as big as a Comanche in here before. Only a couple of weeks ago a Cessna—much lighter than your plane—never got off the ground.' So saying, he pointed to a pile of débris among the trees at the upper end of the runway.

Arnold and I always took it in turns to captain the aircraft and fly from the left-hand seat. Today was my turn. I paced out the runway—1,500 ft. Because of the elevation of the field which was about 5,700 ft above sea-level, the warm climate, and the muddy ground, I knew my take-off run would be greatly increased and that it would be touch and go whether I would make it. (According to the aircraft handbook just over 1,500 ft of dry concrete runway is required to get a Comanche airborne at this altitude.) It was essential to make the aircraft as light as possible. We took out all our baggage and survival equipment and this, together with the fact that our fuel-tanks were half empty, greatly reduced the take-off weight. Nevertheless, to keep the load to an absolute minimum, I determined to make the attempt alone. Lieutenant Bayldon, who the night before had been disappointed at being unable to arrest us as mercenaries, kindly offered to take the others and all our baggage to Mwinilunga by Land Rover.

Old Dr Hoyth, wearing shorts and an open-neck shirt, was standing in front of the Comanche holding his handkerchief out to see which way the wind was blowing. As I climbed into the aircraft he remarked cheerily: 'Well there is only one way to see if you can get her off the ground!'

Not over-eager to join the wrecked Cessna among the trees at the top end of the runway, I decided to take off in the direction of the gentle downward slope. Although this meant I would have a light tail-wind for take-off, it had the important advantage that at the bottom end of the runway the ground broke away and there were no trees to be cleared. I started the engine and after letting it warm up I taxied to the top end of the runway. The ground was so muddy that I got stuck trying to turn the Comanche around. All the village, black and white alike, had turned out to watch, and in no time dozens of eager hands had swung the aircraft round into position. It was with greater thoroughness than ever that I did my take-off checks. I ran the engine up to 2,000 r.p.m., checked the two magnetos individually to make sure the ignition was working properly, pulled back the knob controlling the pitch of the propeller (once to get the oil in the system moving and a second time to check the change on the oil-pressure gauge) and then I pulled the power right back to see that the engine would idle smoothly. This done, I set the power at 1,000 r.p.m. to prevent the sparking-plugs oiling up, and tightened the friction-nut on the throttle control. After checking the flying controls and setting the trim-tab on the elevators, I made sure that the mixture control was set, carburettor heat off, pitch-control knob screwed tight, fuel switched on, correct tank selected, sufficient fuel remaining, fuel booster pump on, fuel pressure adequate, flaps up, engine gauges checked, turn and bank indicator and rotating-beacon on, door locked and safety-belt fastened. With the brakes applied, I gently pushed the throttle control to its forward limit. A confident full-throated roar began to come from the engine. I waited three or four seconds while it developed full power, gave a 'thumbs-up' sign to Arnold who was standing by the right wing of the aircraft, and then released the brakes. As the Comanche gathered speed the mass of black and white people waving from the side of the runway became blurred. I kept one eye on the airspeed indicator, the other on a pile of wood towards the end of the runway on the left-hand side. From my reconnaissance on foot I knew I had to be airborne by the time I reached the pile of wood, for after that there was a continuous patch of mud, beyond which lay a ditch. The airspeed indicator which had at first swung round rapidly seemed to be stuck at 55 m.p.h. (the best speed for a short take-off in a Comanche is 85 m.p.h.).

There was a terrible surge and skid each time the aircraft struck patches of mud, and it felt as if the brakes were being applied with great violence. I was almost abeam the pile of wood: still the airspeed was only 55 m.p.h., a good 10 m.p.h. below the stall-speed. I eased back on the stick—nothing happened. The end of the runway was terrifyingly near. I jerked the stick sharply back. The stall-warning light was on but by a miracle the plane bounced off the ground for a split second, just long enough for the speed to increase and for the Comanche's powerful 250 h.p. engine to lift it into the air. I retracted the undercarriage, and as the aircraft climbed away I mopped the sweat off my face with my handkerchief. I circled the field once, rocked the wings and headed south for Mwinilunga at 300 ft above ground-level to stay clear of the low stratus clouds.

It took no more than ten minutes to reach Mwinilunga. I had only just got out of the Comanche when a Dakota of Central African Airways landed and came over to park beside me. Before I even had time to ask the pilot to send a radio message to Salisbury Air Traffic Control to let them know that I had arrived at Mwinilunga he told me: 'Salisbury lost contact with you last night and they were wondering if you had got here safely. I've already let them know you're okay.' It was fortunate that I had reached Mwinilunga before the Dakota, otherwise a full-scale search and rescue operation might have been set in hand. The pilot, when I told him that I had arrived only just before him, asked where I had spent the night. He had never heard of Sakeji School. But he asked me to mark the airstrip on his map in case he ever needed to make a forced landing there. Doubtless to make me feel better about what had happened the day before, he confessed that even though he had been flying in this part of the world for several years, he still sometimes got lost when trying to find Mwinilunga. Coming from a professional these words were a comfort.

As we were talking, two trucks drove up to the Dakota and some men began unloading the aircraft's cargo of refrigerated meat. The pilot explained that these men were Belgians working for the Union Minière and that the meat was on its way to Kolwezi. Sometimes he had flown up loads of frozen carcasses as often as twice a day from Ndola. When he said that he would be coming up again the next day I mentioned that I was rather short of fuel. He wrote down the number of my Shell credit-card and promised to bring a 25 gallon drum on his next flight up.

The Belgians, after unloading the consignment of meat, gave me a lift into the nearby village of Mwinilunga where there were several heavy trucks all ready to leave in convoy for Kolwezi. They told me that the journey through the jungle would take between eight and twenty-two hours depending on the condition of the track after the rains. When I asked if there would be room on the convoy for my three friends and myself, they eyed me suspiciously and enquired if I were an American. On learning that I was

English, their manner at once became more friendly and not only did they offer to delay their departure until my friends arrived from Sakeji, but they said they would lay on an extra vehicle so that none of us would have to sit in the back of the trucks on the frozen carcasses of beef. I tried to find out the cause of their bitterness against the United States, for it was abundantly clear that had our party not all been Europeans there would have been no room for us on the convoy. It seems they were convinced that the only possible motive the United States could have for enabling the United Nations to destroy such a staunch anti-Communist as Tshombe was so as to rob the Common Market of the mineral wealth of Katanga. They compared it to the United States' attempt to push Britain out of the Middle East so as to give the great U.S. oil companies a share in the oil of the Persian Gulf. I told them that this was altogether too cynical a view of the motives of the United States.

VIII

TSHOMBE'S LAST STAND

THE SITUATION IN Kolwezi was literally explosive. One hundred and ten metric tons of T.N.T. had been removed by the Katangese gendarmerie (as Tshombe's African soldiers were called) from the stocks of the Union Minière and had been attached in generous quantities to all the major installations in the town. High explosives had been placed on the nearby Delcommune Dam and officials of the Union Minière told us that if these were detonated, hundreds of thousands of people living on the river banks below the dam would be killed by the unleashed flood of water that would burst from the reservoir. Some asserted that the surge of water would flood the capitals of Brazzaville and Leopoldville nearly 2,000 miles downstream near the mouth of the Congo River.

Tshombe's position had been militarily untenable since the defeat of his gendarmerie by the U.N. forces at the key town of Jadotville on 3 January 1963, two weeks before our arrival in Kolwezi. The last card remaining in his hand was the threat to destroy the economic potential of an important part of Katanga and to bring large-scale destruction to the Congo. The U.N. troops, regardless of this threat, were advancing and had announced their intention of attacking Kolwezi by the end of the week unless Tshombe surrendered.

It was in the early hours of Wednesday, 16 January that the convoy on which we were travelling eventually rolled into Kolwezi after nearly ten hours on the muddy, bumpy track that winds up through the jungle from Rhodesia into Katanga.

The atmosphere in the city was uncanny. Fear was abroad in the streets. None knew what the next few hours might bring. Would Tshombe surrender? Or, when he knew he could no longer win, would he blow everything up? The only person who knew the answer to this question was Tshombe himself who was holding a meeting of his cabinet that morning at the temporary Presidency. Meanwhile the streets were deserted. The shutters of the houses were closed and the windows boarded up. Kolwezi's 4,000 Belgian inhabitants, many of them women and children, remained for the most part indoors. Rumours were current of atrocities committed by U.N. soldiers during the capture of Elizabethville on 30 December 1962 and there was general apprehension at the prospect of an attack by an army of Irish, Ethiopians, Indians and Indonesians. Added to this was the fear that Tshombe's gendarmerie might panic and run amok, as the U.N. forces drew near. Nor was there any chance of evacuating the women and children to Northern Rhodesia, for the Katangese gendarmes had set up check-points on the roads and would let no one leave the country without the written permission of the Katangese government. The Belgians who had braved the chaos and turmoil of the previous two years in the Congo, seemed resigned to whatever further scourge Fate might choose to afflict them with.

Arnold and I made our way to the Presidency, an undistin-

Kolwezi: President Tshombe and author
OVERLEAF: *woman mourner at funeral*

guished suburban villa which Tshombe had made his headquarters. The cabinet meeting was just breaking up as we
arrived. Godefroid Munongo, the Minister of the Interior and
Tshombe's lieutenant, was the first to leave followed by the other
members of the cabinet. Last to appear was Tshombe who was on
his way to visit his troops. His features were tense but controlled.
As he climbed into his car he shouted to one of his *aides*: 'Enter-
rez les morts.'

It soon became clear to what he had been referring when a
hearse escorted by soldiers of the gendarmerie and followed by
a crowd of wailing women appeared in the avenue outside the
Presidency. We followed the procession which made its way
slowly through the town until it stopped before a Catholic
church where a considerable crowd had gathered. There, two
coffins decked in flowers were unloaded and carried into the
church. The coffins were preceded by a small African boy dressed
in white, who held a cross before him as he made his way up the
aisle between two lines of soldiers presenting arms with their
loaded rifles. It was a curious scene. The service was conducted in
Latin by an African priest. A company of white nuns in a balcony
above the entrance sang the hymns and responses. But when it
came to the Lord's Prayer which was said in French everyone in
the packed church joined in. Even the Katangese soldiers, their
heads bowed, mumbled the words into the muzzles of their guns.

Not until later did we discover how these two heroes of the
Katangese army had met their death. It appears they had been
driving a truck along a road near Kolwezi when a Saab jet of the
U.N. force had passed low overhead. In panic they had leapt
from their moving vehicle, fracturing their skulls as they hit the
ground.

From the church, Arnold and I went to the Union Minière
headquarters, where we tried to get permission to see over the

Kolwezi: 'Christian', a soldier of fortune
OVERLEAF: *Bob Denier, Katangese mercenary commander*

Delcommune Dam. But an assistant general manager of the company M. Gonze, a Belgian, explained that far from being able to give us permission, company officials were not even allowed near the dam which had been completely taken over by the Katangese gendarmerie. He told us that he had been unable to prevent the gendarmerie commandeering the company's stock of high explosives which had been kept for use in the mines. 'Do you think we want to have our plants and equipment blown up?' he asked plaintively. Of the twelve hydro-electric turbines operated by the Delcommune Dam, only one was working; the other eleven all had charges attached to them, ready to be blown up at a minute's notice. It was believed that the charges had been set by a South African explosives expert and, to the dismay of the Union Minière, it was reported that he had done his job well.

We lunched at a hostel near the centre of town called the Bonne Auberge. It lived up to its name. Arnold and I had two of the most tender steaks we had ever eaten—we concluded that the ten hours of bouncing and banging on the road from Mwinilunga the night before had had a more beneficial effect on the beef carcasses than on our own. In the course of the meal my eye was caught by a strange sight the other side of the glass swing-doors of the restaurant. Standing in the hallway was a figure dressed in camouflage battle-dress with a large-calibre revolver slung under the arm in a shoulder-holster; and hanging from underneath a khaki bush-hat were two long blonde pig-tails. A visitor to Africa soon becomes accustomed to seeing unusual things, but I confess I had to look twice to believe my eyes. It turned out that this Amazon was a Madame Yvette who with her husband Alex, a German from Byelo-Russia, had been through the Algerian War. She told us that they had both just arrived in the Congo to fight as mercenaries in Tshombe's army.

In the afternoon we visited a small villa in the outskirts of

Kolwezi where some of the mercenaries had established their headquarters. Outside the house, stacked up haphazardly against the wall, were cases of ammunition, belts of heavy machine-gun bullets, a few three-inch mortars and several boxes of mortar-bombs. Half a dozen mercenaries, most of them Belgians, were relaxing on the porch in deck-chairs. The mercenaries, knowing that the hours of Katanga's secession from the Congo were numbered, were discussing where they could find future employment in the same line of business. One suggested Laos, another Burundi, while a third called Christian thought the National Congolese Army was a possibility. 'After all,' he observed, 'they too need European officers.'

The mercenaries are a strange race of people. Each has a story to tell; and that of Christian was in many ways typical. (To conceal their identities, many of the mercenaries use only their first names.) A wiry, soft-spoken Belgian in his middle thirties, Christian was proud of the fact that he had been one of the first Belgians to join the Hitler Youth Movement at the beginning of World War II. He had subsequently travelled to the Far East as a member of a jazz band and had eventually ended up as a clerk working for a Belgian shipping line in Leopoldville, the capital of the Congo. There an unhappy love-affair had induced him to make three attempts at suicide. When all three attempts proved unsuccessful he concluded he had a charmed life and decided to become a mercenary in Tshombe's army. He told us that he enjoyed the job which earned him £350 per month paid into a bank in Belgium.

In action the mercenaries operated in groups of two or three, with a dozen or more Katangese soldiers under them. They usually took up a defensive position, waited until the U.N. troops were within range, let off a few mortar-bombs and some bursts of machine-gun fire—then they ran. It seems that they were good

runners for during the whole Congo operation no more than a
handful of mercenaries were killed in action. Until the week before
our arrival in Kolwezi there had been more than one hundred
mercenaries in Katanga. But with Tshombe's fortunes waning,
half of these had already left for Angola and Northern Rhodesia.
The remainder were preparing to follow.

Tshombe's mercenaries were a grave political liability for him
in the eyes of the world. But Katanga, within days of declaring its
independence in July 1961, had found itself having to defend its
new-found sovereignty against both the Congolese Army and
the U.N. forces. Faced with the necessity of rapidly expanding the
small Katangese army, Tshombe, like the leaders of many other
Afro-Asian states including the Congo itself, hired foreigners to
train and officer his army. However, by no means all the Europeans who fought for Tshombe were mercenaries. Many, particularly those who lived in Katanga, believed that the United
Nations had come to the Congo not to represent the cause of
Justice, but to represent the political interest of the Afro-Asian
nations. They felt that its duty was to re-establish order in the
rest of the Congo, not to spread chaos and destruction to the
one part of the Congo where order had been maintained. Thus
when the Katangese made a stand against the advance of the
U.N. forces, it is not surprising that many Europeans volunteered
to fight beside them, and it is ironical that the United Nations,
which complained so bitterly about Tshombe's soldiers of fortune, should have employed even more mercenaries than did the
Katangese. For, fighting with the U.N. forces on behalf of India,
were the tough Nepalese Gurkhas—the most famous and formidable mercenaries in the world today. (There is still a brigade of
Gurkha troops in the British Army and in the early part of 1964
there were several Gurkha units in action in North Borneo and
Sarawak resisting the incursions of Indonesian guerillas into

Malaysian territory.) The trouble was that Tshombe's mercenaries had the wrong-coloured skins.

By the time Arnold and I returned to the Presidency later in the day, Tshombe had made up his mind and it was announced that he would be flying to Elizabethville the next day to meet one of U Thant's representatives. The Katangan President had many times before had talks with the United Nations, more with a view to playing for time than in the hope that an agreement could be reached that was satisfactory to both the Katangese and the United Nations. Indeed the whole Congo operation was characterized by successive bouts of fighting and talking. It must have been Tshombe's hope that if the grisly affair could be dragged out long enough, the United Nations would become either bored or bankrupt, and go away. For some time there had been growing apprehension in New York at the mounting cost of the operation. Already, more than a year before, Ghana, Guinea, Indonesia, Morocco, Sudan, Mali, Tunisia and the U.A.R., countries that had been among the foremost in demanding Tshombe's destruction, had withdrawn part or all of their forces from the Congo. But Tshombe, in supposing that the United Nations would pack its bags and go home, had misjudged the extent of the Afro-Asians' hatred of him and the determination of the United States Government to champion the Afro-Asian cause. Now, after more than two and a half years Tshombe had nothing left to negotiate. Only a small part of Katanga remained under his control and his threat to blow everything up was never anything more than a threat, for he had no desire to inflict more devastation and destruction on his country than had already been done by the United Nations. Tshombe knew that to go to Elizabethville the next day meant surrender.

Arnold and I decided to get back to Elizabethville in time to witness the last chapter in Tshombe's bid to establish an independent state of Katanga. We learned from the Union Minière that a convoy would be setting out at 4.30 the following morning for Mwinilunga where we had left our plane. There would be room for us, but we were warned that it was essential to have an exit-permit from the Government if we were to be allowed through the Katangese road-blocks.

Shortly after 10 p.m. we returned to the Presidency to procure the necessary exit-permits. We were told that a cabinet meeting was being held and that it would be some time before we would get our permits. We decided to wait, and sat down on the grass verge of the driveway within fifteen feet of the entrance to the Presidency which was guarded by a stocky Katangese gendarme. As we sat in the darkness we could see through the white muslin curtains into the drawing-room where Tshombe was talking to members of his cabinet. Suddenly, above the low murmur of voices from the room, we heard the brisk tramp of boots entering the driveway. Bob Denier, the chief mercenary, a solid 6 ft 6 in. Belgian with an enormous red moustache whom we recognized from our visit to the mercenaries' villa earlier in the day, appeared with two of his comrades. All three were carrying their submachine guns at the ready. They marched swiftly to the entrance of the Presidency. Denier pushed aside the dumbfounded Katangese guard and kicked open the door which gave immediately onto the room where Tshombe and his ministers were sitting. The mercenaries took up positions in two corners of the room covering everybody there with their menacing weapons. It was impossible to hear what was being said, but through the veiled windows we could see that Tshombe had got to his feet and was walking agitatedly up and down the room. It immediately occurred to us that this was a last minute attempt by the mercenaries to prevent Tshombe surrendering the next day. The squeal of brakes interrupted our thoughts and speculations. Half a dozen jeeps carrying the rest of the mercenaries had drawn up in the road outside. Inside the grounds of the Presidency Tshombe's Katangese guard, forty strong, became alarmed. In the darkness there was the snap of a rifle being cocked, rapidly followed by others. One of the mercenaries shouted in French from outside in the roadway: 'If they don't let Bob and the others out unharmed, we'll kill every black in the place.'

Arnold and I sitting between the mercenaries and the Katangese, began to feel a trifle uncomfortable. This was one way to get ourselves an exit-visa from Katanga, but not quite the one we had planned. We edged over into the shadow of Tshombe's large black limousine in the hope that it would afford us at least some cover, if the lead were to start flying.

After several long minutes, Denier reappeared. As he strode out of the Presidency he commented calmly: 'Nothing unusual— just a slight misunderstanding.' The mercenaries disappeared into the night as quickly as they had come. An uneasy silence fell on the sleeping town of Kolwezi. As far as we could learn the incident arose from a dispute between the mercenaries and Tshombe's gendarmerie; nevertheless it is illustrative of the ease with which a handful of determined men in this part of the world can hold a government at their mercy. In this case a loyal guard of forty soldiers, taken by surprise, had looked on paralysed as three men held their chief at gun-point. There is little likelihood of Communists gaining control of an African country by popular vote. But the danger that does exist and that will long plague the nations of Africa, comes from the facility with which a few ruthless and well-trained men can overthrow a government. The most recent example of this has been the revolution in Zanzibar in January 1964 when a handful of thugs under their Cuban-trained leader, 'Field-Marshal' Okello, were able to gain control of the island within a month of its gaining its independence.

Although at the time of writing it looks as if power on the island has passed into the hands of Sheik Abeid Karume, the African nationalist leader, and it is possible that the Tanganyika-Zanzibar link-up announced in April 1964 will strengthen his position.

In the early hours of the morning we left Kolwezi with the Union Minière convoy, having eventually obtained the necessary passes signed by M. Yav, the Katangese Defence Minister, and General Muké, the Commander-in-Chief. When we reached Mwinilunga Airport we found that the Central African Airways pilot I had met two days before had left a 25 gallon drum of fuel beside our aircraft, as he had promised. Using a short length of rubber pipe and after getting several mouthfuls of petrol, we were able to siphon the fuel into the Comanche's tanks. We then left for Elizabethville where Tshombe had arrived earlier in the day. We were at the U.N. building in time to see him emerge from his talks with Mr George Sherry of the United Nations. Tshombe tried bravely to raise a smile, but his rule over an independent Katanga was at an end.

It is ironic that a man who seemingly represented the Western ideals of self-determination and racial tolerance and who was a staunch anti-Communist should have been destroyed by the West itself. His crime was that he had appeared to be too pro-West. In the eyes of the Afro-Asian nations he was a 'capitalist stooge' and a 'pawn of neo-colonialism'. However, it would appear that Tshombe's loyalty was not to the Union Minière, but to Katanga and himself—not necessarily in that order. He seized the opportunity presented by the disorders in the Congo to secede and declare Katanga's independence. There is little evidence to suggest that he took this action as a result of promptings from the Union Minière. The Union Minière, by its own claim, had no choice but to co-operate; be that as it may, it is clear that it was no unwilling partner of Tshombe's ambition. It perhaps thought that the Katangese leader would be easier to do business with than the remote Leopoldville government which might prove less amenable to Union Minière interests. The Union Minière's paramount concern was to keep its mines working. A pre-requisite of this was the maintenance of law and order and it would seem that the Union Minière believed this could be better done by Tshombe than by a Central Congolese Government some 1,500 miles away whose difficulties seemed insuperable.

The problems to be faced in ruling the Congo, a country whose three major cities are as far apart as London, Algiers and Budapest, are enormous. Dense tropical jungles cover the greater part of the country and obstruct all but air communications. The Congo has never had any historical unity; it was drawn on the map of Africa by nineteenth century European statesmen who, with neither knowledge of the land nor of the people, were intent only on carving up the continent of Africa between themselves. In a country like this where numerous tribes speaking different languages are cut off politically, economically and geographically from one another, there cannot but be strong separatist tendencies. Separatism is not a theory, as some would suppose, cooked up by the Union Minière to suit its own convenience. It is a clear fact. The only thread of unity in the whole of this vast territory is the Congo River which, with its great tributaries, was the only means of getting about the country until the advent of the aeroplane. And not even the Congo River reaches effectively into the highland plateau of Katanga, a province by itself twice the size of West Germany. Nor was Katanga alone in having strong separatist tendencies; with the breakdown of the Central Government in July 1960, these became evident in two other of the Congo's six provinces, Kivu and Kasai. In addition to the problem of separatism, the Congo has to face the woe that besets all the under-developed countries of the world—the mass misery of its

people. In all these countries poverty creates a great well of discontent; and it is this that is the chief cause of political unrest all
over the globe. Because of the recent chaos in the Congo the
situation is worse there than in most other African countries although nothing like as bad as in some parts of the Far East such
as India or China. (India, a country approximately the same size
as the Congo, supports, albeit precariously, a population more
than thirty times as great: 450 million as against 14 million.)
Wherever there is large-scale discontent the standard of revolt is
easily raised. This is particularly true of the Congo where rebels
can swiftly vanish into the jungle at the approach of government
forces. In early 1964 widespread havoc was created in Kwilu
Province, immediately to the east of Leopoldville, by Peking-
trained Pierre Mulele, a former minister of education in Lumumba's
government, who was leading a revolt of the Jeunesse (Youth)
Party against the Central Government. It was reported that more
than 100 local government officials had been killed and some 150
villages burned to the ground; yet the Central Government
seemed unable to call a halt to the disorders.

The separatism and anarchy that are endemic in the Congo
conspire to make the Central Government's task an impossible
one. And it remains to be seen whether the political settlement imposed on Katanga by the United Nations at the cost of
more than £150 million can be maintained now that the U.N.
forces have been withdrawn.* The United Nations did not have
the resources to remain indefinitely in the Congo. Soon after
Tshombe's capitulation in January 1963 the U.N. force was cut
from 19,000 men to 7,000, and it was intended that these should

* On 6 July 1964 within a week of the departure of the last U.N. soldiers
from the Congo, President Kasabubu called upon M. Tshombe to form a
government, following the resignation of M. Adoula. And on 10 July 1964,
only one day short of the fourth anniversary of his declaration of Katangese
independence, Tshombe became Prime Minister of the Congo Republic.

be withdrawn by the end of 1963. But apprehension that Premier Adoula's government might lose control prompted U Thant to agree that they should remain a further six months at a cost of £6·5 million, a sum greater than the United Nations' total budget for civil operations in one year. The last U.N. soldiers left the Congo on 30 June 1964 and now all depends, as it did in July 1960, on the Leopoldville government's ability to maintain order in the country. It will be a commendable feat if General Mobutu is able to retrain and discipline the 30,000-strong Congolese Army sufficiently to do its job and to avoid a repetition of the mutiny which followed independence and which set off the whole Congo crisis.

The crises in both the Yemen and the Congo have made it clear that the Western Alliance is deeply divided on the basic issue of how to arrest the spread of Communism throughout the world. The United States, by its recognition of the Egyptian-supported Republican Government of the Yemen and by continuing its economic aid to the United Arab Republic, has given tacit approval to Egyptian aggression against its smaller neighbour. And in the Congo, the United States not only condoned the imposition of a political settlement by force on Katanga, but provided the economic backing without which it could not have been effected. Britain, on the other hand, has refused to approve Egypt's flagrant act of aggression in the Yemen and has been reluctant to see military intervention by foreign troops in the Congo to impose a political settlement. There is much to be said for Britain's policy of non-intervention in both the Yemen and the Congo, provided such a policy is coupled with an all-out effort to prevent other nations from intervening. However in both these disputes the United States, in company with the Afro-Asian nations, has been on the side of intervention. Many Europeans believe that it is a fear of being put in the same pillory as the former colonial powers that has prompted the United States not only to appease Afro-Asian demands, but to seek to become the champion of their cause. Be this as it may, it is evident that the United States State Department believes that the interests of the West can best be served by supporting Nationalism the world over (with the possible exception of the Western Hemisphere). That this is the best policy has yet to be proved. The countries of Europe still prefer respect to popularity. One of the advantages of the split in the Western Alliance over the Congo crisis was that with the United States on one side and Belgium, France and Britain rather half-heartedly on the other, there was no side for the Russians to be on.

IX

LAND OF THE PIONEERS

THE INSIGNIFICANT STREAM that babbles by Sakeji School gently turning the missionaries' small water-wheel, soon grows into the great Zambezi River and, after a tortuous 700 mile southward journey, affords the most breath-taking spectacle in all of Africa—the Victoria Falls. As we approached by air we were surprised to see a large white cloud resting on the ground ahead of us. The fact that it was a cloudless day made the sight all the more remarkable. Only when we got closer did we realize that the cloud was hanging over the Falls and was made of spray thrown up hundreds of feet into the air by the fury of the Zambezi waters plunging headlong into the gorge below. Once over the Falls we banked the Comanche steeply so that the cauldron of seething, steaming waters seemed to hang from our wing-tip. Fascinated by the sight, we circled the Falls two or three times before coming in to land at the nearby airstrip where we were curtly informed that the minimum height over the Falls was 2,000 ft, not 200 ft as we had supposed.

The Victoria Falls, discovered by David Livingstone, the Scottish missionary, in 1855 during his trans-continental journey of exploration, are broader than those at Niagara and more than twice the height (354 ft as against 175 ft). Livingstone, like so many explorers of his day, called his discovery after the British sovereign. But the Falls are known to the local Africans by a much more descriptive name: 'The smoke that thunders'. They have named it well for the roar of the waters can be heard for miles around and standing near the gorge the ground trembles beneath one's feet.

There are numerous vantage points from which the Falls may be seen, one more dramatic than the other. Several times, as we watched from the precipitous edge of the chasm, the wind changed and we were drenched by a shower of spray. In places where the spray falls continuously the dense jungle of a tropical rain-forest has grown up. One could spend hours watching the ever-changing rainbows that hang suspended in the cloud of spray overhead. And the sight of two million gallons of water per second leaping into thin air and crashing down into the chasm below with a thunderous roar exercises a gripping fascination. Most onlookers stand spellbound before the power of Nature, but others, less easily impressed, remark like the dour Scotsman on being shown Niagara: 'And what's to prevent it?'

I had a letter of introduction to a young Rhodesian called Timothy Braybrooke who was a ranger (or warden) at the Wankie Game Reserve which borders on the Zambezi and covers some 5,000 square miles. He and his wife would not hear of us going to the nearby hotel and invited Arnold and myself to stay with them at Zambezi Camp which stands by the river a few miles up-stream from the Falls. Braybrooke had a speed-boat which he used to police the river and prevent poachers getting into the Reserve from Northern Rhodesia on the other side of the Zambezi.

And during our two-day stay he took us on a patrol up the river. In spite of its great width and a calmness more suggestive of a mill-pond, the Zambezi is fast-flowing. Not far upstream the seeming placidity of the river is broken by rapids. Here the waters foam and boil as they rush over shallow boulders. Great troughs furrow the troubled surface in the lee of each submerged rock and whirlpools curl viciously round those that protrude from the waters. As it struck rough patches the boat was tossed about and I fully expected a rock to burst through the thin wooden hull at any minute. The hippopotamuses sun-bathing in the back-waters stared blankly at us out of one eye, then finding even this too much of an effort they would yawn disinterestedly in best hippopotamus style and sink beneath the surface, only to re-emerge a little later with no more than their noses out of the water. Doubtless, lurking on the muddy banks darkly shaded by the hectic tangle of jungle, there were other eyes watching our progress up the rapids with less benevolence but greater interest, ready to slither into the waters to retrieve whatever might be palatable from a wreck. But Braybrooke knew the river well and we made our way at full speed dodging the submerged rocks with great dexterity (or perhaps even greater luck) until after about fifteen miles we were unable to go any further and returned in the direction of the Falls. Just above the Falls the river broadens to meander among a maze of islands of luxuriant greenness as if to delay its plunge into the chasm whose warning roar builds to a deafening crescendo as the innocent-looking lip of the Falls is approached.

After two relaxing days at Victoria Falls it was time to get on our way once more and we took off full of regret that we did not have time to take Braybrooke up on his offer to show us over the Wankie Game Reserve. From the Falls we followed the east-ward course of the Zambezi until it flowed into Lake Kariba, the largest man-made lake in the world (at least until Lake Nasser is filled). The power-house below the Kariba Dam supplies electricity to Northern Rhodesia's Copper Belt and Southern Rhodesia's light industries, as well as to the civilian population of both territories. After overflying the dam we turned south towards Salisbury, the capital of Southern Rhodesia.

In 1891 my great-grandfather Lord Randolph Churchill, temporarily fed up with politics at home and drawn by the 'attractions of travel, of the chase, and specially of seeking gold for oneself', (Lord Randolph Churchill: *Men, Mines and Animals in South Africa*) had made an expedition to Southern Rhodesia, or Mashonaland as it was then known. The journey from England which took him seventeen weeks, can today be accomplished in fewer hours; although it had taken us, stopping in eighteen countries on the way, all of ten weeks. In those days it was a journey that was neither easy nor comfortable. The voyage to Cape Town took him three weeks, during the course of which the small steamer in which he travelled passed through the oppressive heat of the tropics, met heavy seas and, shortly before reaching its destination, caught on fire. At that time the railway line from the Cape reached as far as Vryburg on the edge of the Boer Republic of the Transvaal, 150 miles north of Kimberley where Lord Randolph broke his journey to visit the diamond mines which had recently been amalgamated by Cecil Rhodes into the De Beers Company and which were by then producing some £2 million of diamonds annually. From Vryburg it was a four-day ride by horse-drawn coach to Johannesburg which had grown in only five years to become a prosperous town of 15,000 inhabitants, following the discovery of gold on the Witwatersrand. The Rand, as it came to be called, was already yielding £2,500,000 worth of gold each year and was fast becoming the world's richest goldfield. However, it was not until the Limpopo River was crossed

and the Transvaal left behind, that the difficult part of the journey began. Thereafter it was the story of the Old Frontier, little
different in southern Africa from what it had been in the Wild
West of America only a few years before. It was the land of the
pioneers: the land of opportunity. Dragging their ox-carts through
raging torrents, crossing wild and desolate plains, enduring hardship and braving the hostility of tribes in their path, they pressed
resolutely onwards determined that they should come to a Promised Land. There were rumours of gold in Mashonaland which
was reputed to be the land of King Solomon's Mines and these
men, escaping the humdrum routine of daily life, had come to
make their fortunes. It took Lord Randolph's expedition six weeks
to cover the 400 miles from Fort Tuli, on the banks of the Limpopo, to Fort Salisbury their destination. On the way the wag-
gons got stuck in the fast-flowing stream of the Wanetse river
and crossing the dry grassland on their way to the high veldt
the expedition only narrowly escaped destruction by a veldt fire.
By the time Fort Salisbury was reached, four out of thirteen horses
and thirteen out of twenty mules had died of 'horse sickness';
besides this two of the oxen had broken their necks falling into a
gully and another had strayed. Nevertheless Lord Randolph concluded: 'I had been exceptionally fortunate.'

Fort Salisbury had been founded less than a year before his
arrival. In 1890 Rhodes had organized an expedition from South
Africa up to the high veldt, the land of the Matabele Zulus; he
had heard about the country from a hunter named Selous who
had made several safaris to the area around Mount Hampden, a
hill that rises to 500 ft out of a flat and fertile plain. The expedition
had split in two: one part had headed east to forestall a Portuguese
advance from Mozambique, while the other had made direct for
Mount Hampden to build an advance post there. This latter
group however, mistaking a smaller hill twelve miles to the west

for Mount Hampden, had already begun construction before it
was realized that this had not been the spot intended by Rhodes
for the new post. Thus Salisbury was founded by accident. Already within a year the place 'was becoming quite a township,
with a regular street of huts and tents, possessing two auc-
tioneers'. (The latter, presumably employees of Rhodes's British
South Africa Chartered Company, were leasing off areas of land
to pioneers and speculators.) And Lord Randolph remarked that
it had 'a thriving, rising, healthy appearance'.

Today, more than seventy years later, my great-grandfather's
comment on Salisbury still holds good, at least at first sight. To
the traveller arriving from the north, who has passed through the
squalor of Cairo and observed the dingy Indian-style buildings
that abound in Nairobi, the Southern Rhodesian capital is the
most impressive city he has seen since leaving the Mediterranean.
The 'huts and tents' of the pioneers have given way to giant skyscrapers and modern office-blocks. The one 'regular street' has
blossomed into broad tree-lined avenues—Rhodes had insisted
that they be wide enough for an eight-pair team of oxen to be
turned around with ease. The city, standing in a fertile and sunny
plain nearly 5,000 ft above sea-level, enjoys a pleasantly warm,
yet invigorating climate. It wears the face of prosperity and might
for all the world be a boom-town of the American Middle West.

But appearances are deceptive. A closer look at the large office-
blocks reveals signs in the windows that read 'To be Let'. And
compared to the hustle and noise one associates with a boom-
town, the streets seem strangely deserted. The fact is, Salisbury's
boom is ended. In spite of extravagant rumours and high hopes,
the pioneers of the 1890's never made a rich gold strike. Lord
Randolph had been as sanguine as anyone about the prospects
of finding gold and, in conjunction with Mr Alfred Beit, he had
purchased a half-share in the 'Matchless' mine near Hartley Hill,

some fifty miles south-west of Salisbury. Nevertheless, after spending just over two months visiting mines in the area around Salisbury, sometimes in the company of Cecil Rhodes, he admitted: 'The truth has to be told. Mashonaland, so far as it is at present known, and much is known, is neither an Arcadia nor an El Dorado.' But he adds: 'If Fort Salisbury should ever become an important township, farms here might be very profitable. I came across two enterprising persons who had each in attractive spots marked out the regulation area of three thousand acres, and were busily engaged in erecting huts. They seemed confident of success, and were in excellent spirits.' Lord Randolph was again right. For when it became evident that there was little gold in Southern Rhodesia, many of the pioneers who had come in on the get-rich-quick spree were prepared to settle for a farm. And those that followed came to peg out a piece of land for cultivation rather than to stake a claim to a mine. Today agriculture is the country's chief source of wealth, through its export of tobacco.

Although it had always been mildly prosperous, it was not until the Central African Federation came into being in 1953 that Salisbury's boom began. Economically federation was a sensible idea. It would link Northern Rhodesia, with its rich Copper Belt, providing 15 per cent of the world copper production and accounting for £130 million worth of exports annually; Nyasaland, with its great well of industrious and competent African labour; and Southern Rhodesia which, with its tobacco growing, chrome production and light industries, would provide sufficient diversification so that the Federation's prosperity would not depend solely on the maintenance of a high world price for copper. With these bright prospects for the future Salisbury real-estate values soared, as did a mass of prestige buildings. The Federation seemed set on the high-road to prosperity.

Yet, within ten years the experiment had proved a failure. And by the end of 1963 the Central African Federation had ceased to exist and the Federal Prime Minister Sir Roy Welensky found himself out of a job. Although the idea had been economically sound, federation had never been viable politically. Few Africans were consulted in the matter and the vast majority of those able to understand what was going on were violently opposed to the idea, believing that federation was a political device to give the European a longer lease of dominance in Central Africa. This was particularly felt in Nyasaland, where the ratio of blacks to whites in 1962 was 332 to 1, and in Northern Rhodesia 32 to 1, compared to only 16 to 1 in Southern Rhodesia where the European seemed to be more firmly in the seat of power. The growth of vocal nationalist parties in Nyasaland under Dr Hastings Banda and in Northern Rhodesia under Dr Kenneth Kaunda, coupled with the successes of African Nationalism elsewhere in the continent, has led to the abandonment of federation. On 6 July 1964 Nyasaland became independent under the name of Malawi and Northern Rhodesia, to be known as Zambia, follows suit on 24 October 1964. This leaves only Southern Rhodesia with its 220,000 Europeans who comprised four-fifths of the total European population of the former Federation. There also, nationalist parties are growing, under Mr Joshua Nkomo and the Rev. Ndabaninge Sithole. But the Rhodesian Front Party which has the backing of the majority of Europeans seems determined to maintain European ascendancy as long as it is able to do so.

'Unlike Kenya which came into being as the rich man's playground where people came to shoot animals and everyone slept with everyone else's wife, Rhodesia was founded by small-time farmers of Scottish and Afrikaans origin who arrived, Bible in one hand, spade in the other, to colonize the land.' This explanation from a Rhodesian farmer perhaps accounts for the continued existence of a colour-bar in Southern Rhodesia. In Kenya, which was to become independent only a few months after our visit, prudence had dictated the ending of racial discrimination, although the settlers' Muthaiga Club by the time of our departure had not yet seen fit to open its doors to Africans (except of course as servants). However, even before the threat of independence, the colour-bar in Kenya was never as strict as it is in Southern Rhodesia, largely because the Kenya settler was wealthier and more self-assured than his Southern Rhodesian counterpart. This does not go to prove that rich men are better than poor—a doubtful proposition at the best of times. The difference was that in Kenya there was an economic bar that divided the farmers and big ranchers from the African population; therefore they felt little need for a colour-bar as such. It is the people who have to compete with another race for their jobs and for their social and economic position that develop the strongest racial prejudices. And this is true not only of the negro. What about the Jew? For centuries the Jew has been despised by the poorer sections of European society for his adeptness at making money, and still is today. In the wealthier ranks of society this prejudice, while existing all too often, is less deep-rooted and there can be few rich people today (on either side of the Atlantic) who would not be delighted to dine at the table of a Rothschild. In the same way a wealthy rancher in Kenya would have no qualms about dining with an educated African or a tribal chief. Not so the white miners in Northern Rhodesia's Copper Belt or on South Africa's Rand; not so the European farmers in Southern Rhodesia or South Africa—most would sooner die. In the case of the Boers, who form the majority (60 per cent) of the white population in South Africa and an eighth of it in Southern Rhodesia, this prejudice has been heightened by a religious bigotry that leads them to the firm conviction that the negro, like the rest of creation, has been brought into existence by God to be of service to the white man. It must in fairness be stated that there are others, both in southern Africa and in the southern states of America who share this view.

Salisbury provided our first encounter in Africa with the colour-bar. We soon discovered that the hotel in which we were staying would not admit Africans. Cinemas were segregated. Lavatories and elevators in buildings were labelled 'Europeans only'. By the terms of the Land Apportionment Act Africans may only have houses or own shops in specified parts of the city; nor are they allowed to be in the European part of town at night without special passes. Yet, this is the land that by its constitution is committed to, and by its own claim practises, a policy of racial partnership. While there is some argument in favour of denying the vote to someone who is totally ignorant and uneducated, and while the proprietor of a hotel or restaurant might be entitled to deny access to his premises to a person untidily dressed or unable to pay the bill, there is no justification, nor can there ever be one, for saying to a man: 'You cannot come in here because of the colour of your skin.'

One afternoon, while I was sitting writing my diary on the first-floor terrace of the hotel I was staying in, a middle-aged blonde, whom I had disturbed by the clacking of my typewriter, came and sat down nearby. 'Are you a journalist?' she enquired. When I confessed to this, she told me that she was the wife of a politician who had got into Parliament at the last elections as a candidate for the Rhodesian Front Party led by Mr Winston Field. (Field had replaced Sir Edgar Whitehead as Southern Rhodesian Prime Minister, after the latter's United Federal Party had lost the elections. Whitehead, it is thought, alienated many of his supporters when in a pre-election speech he expressed the hope that within ten years the Africans of Southern Rhodesia would have the greater share of political power in the country. While the general idea had been tacitly agreed to by many, if not the majority of the settlers, its statement in concrete terms provoked an outcry—ten years seemed alarmingly close to the Europeans, but disappointingly far off to the Africans.) When the blonde asked me what I thought of 'apartheid' a heated argument ensued, in the course of which, with true feminine logic, she demanded: 'Would you like to have your wife and daughter raped by a black man?' This question is similar to that put from time to time in public-opinion polls designed to show support for a policy of unilateral nuclear disarmament: 'Would you like your family to be exterminated by a hydrogen bomb?' Of course no one wants to have their family exterminated: the method is immaterial. Argument upon these lines is fruitless. And without entering upon the rights and wrongs of 'apartheid', I confined myself to pointing out the short-sightedness of such a policy. For it will be impossible for the European minorities in southern Africa to maintain their political domination indefinitely, whether they are prepared to fight an Algerian War in southern Africa (as Portugal and South Africa seem prepared to do) or not. The longer and more ruthlessly European domination is maintained, the less likely it is that Europeans will be able to remain when eventually African majority governments take over.

The British Government has made it clear that it is not prepared to grant independence to Southern Rhodesia under the terms of its present constitution which excludes by property, income and educational qualifications all but a handful of Africans from any substantial part in the government of their country and is likely to do so for at least the next ten years. Britain's Minister for Commonwealth Relations, Mr Duncan Sandys, has stated that any basis on which Southern Rhodesia might be granted independence must be generally acceptable to the

Commonwealth countries, although this does not mean that advice will either be asked, or listened to, from Ghana's dictator Dr Kwame Nkrumah.

Many suppose that the principle of 'one man—one vote' is the essence of Democracy. This is not true in the case of countries where a large proportion, if not the majority of the electorate is uneducated, illiterate and ill-informed, for in such countries this principle can provide an easy path to tyranny, as witnessed by the sorry state of affairs in Ghana, the first of the African states to become independent in recent years. Posing as the leader of African Nationalism, Ghana has become its worst advertisement. For there, Democracy has become a farce, Justice a mockery and Liberty non-existent. A tyranny, far worse than any endured under British rule, has been established by a jumped-up dictator. Thus, for the benefit and protection of both the African and European populations, it would seem desirable that Southern Rhodesia, before advancing to independence, should be given a modified constitution based on adult suffrage with a minimum educational qualification. This probably would not be the solution favoured by African or European extremists; nevertheless if it could be made to work, it would be the one most likely to ensure a harmonious future for a multi-racial society which, in Southern Rhodesia, is not an ideal, but a fact. Then, with African majority governments in all three territories, it might one day prove possible to reconstitute a Central African Federation.

If the Europeans in Southern Rhodesia fail to realize that the only way they will be able to remain in the country is by handing over the greater part of their political power to the Africans, then they (like the Europeans in Kenya in 1960) must be brought to this realization by the British Government. There is little time to be lost. Fear that motivates the policies of the South African Government, is already creeping into Southern Rhodesia. And

fear is the worst enemy of reason. On our arrival at Mount Hampden Airport near Salisbury the airport manager, a most helpful man, had advised us to lock our aircraft up inside a hangar. Arnold and I had not been in the habit of hangaring the Comanche except when there was a strong wind or blowing sand. We had decided early in the trip that five shillings a night (the average hangarage fee in Africa) for four months was too costly. We had left it out in the open both near the Yemeni border and on the Katangese, and we saw no reason for not doing so in Southern Rhodesia. When I told the airport manager that we would sooner leave the aircraft outside, he pressed me to change my mind, exclaiming: 'There's danger of sabotage!' I thanked him for his advice but explained that we always made a careful check of the aircraft before taking off. We soon heard more about sabotage—railway lines being blown up and petrol bombs being thrown into the homes of both Africans and Europeans. This was allegedly being done by the extreme nationalists in the proscribed Zimbabwe African Peoples Union (ZAPU), who seek to intimidate their own people as well as the Europeans. The fact that European opinion has moved further to the Right with the replacement of Whitehead's United Federal Party by the Rhodesian Front Party, first under Mr Winston Field and more recently under Mr Ian Smith, has induced many Africans to move further to the Left, with a consequent increase in acts of violence and sabotage. As the two political extremes move further apart, tension and fear are bound to grow. If this trend is allowed to continue much longer it may prove too late to retrieve the situation. Hence the need for urgent action by the British Government.

Taxi-drivers are often great philosophers. The African who drove us to the airport as we were leaving Salisbury showed no unwillingness to discuss local politics. He told us he belonged to 'that banned ZAPU'. And when I asked him about segregation he

Johannesburg: new recruits on an East Rand gold mine

said: 'I don't mind being made to live with my own people in an African township. But apartheid is a stupid idea; this country without whites or without blacks would be nothing—we must get together.'

X

WE REACH THE CAPE

By the time we touched down at Johannesburg's Jan Smuts Airport just before dusk, the evening newspapers were already reporting that we had taken off from Salisbury earlier in the day despite the fact that our generator, radios and electrical equipment were all out of action. In these circumstances it was somewhat surprising that the Oppenheimers, who had kindly invited us to stay with them in Johannesburg, had even bothered to send a car to the airport to meet us.

Since the fault (which was later traced to the voltage-regulator) could be more easily rectified in Johannesburg and since our hosts there were expecting us that evening, we had taken off regardless. On our way south we had stopped for a couple of hours at the small airfield of Fort Victoria where we were able to get a taxi and visit the nearby Zimbabwe ruins. These are remarkable in that they are virtually the only noteworthy stone remains of an early civilization to be found on the continent outside of North Africa. The C14 carbon-dating process has established the date of construction as being between the sixth and ninth centuries A.D. So far as is known the ruins are the work of the ancestors of the local Mashona (Bantu) people whose prosperity was based on the sale of gold to India. The tall walls of Zimbabwe are built of blocks of smooth, close-fitting stone held together, so far as one could judge, without any form of mortar. In this respect the stone-work at Zimbabwe bears a remarkable similarity to that at Macchu Picchu, the Lost City of the Incas high in the Andes, which I visited in 1961. As I examined the walls which are linked with gigantic boulders to form a citadel on the crest of a hill, our African taxi-driver who was also filling the office of guide remarked rather wistfully: 'I don't know who built all this, but I don't think it was my people.' It seems he was a victim as I nearly was of settler mythology which, heedless of the scientific facts, asserts that Zimbabwe could never have been built by Africans but must have been the work of 'invaders' from Arabia or India.

Hardly had we landed at Johannesburg Airport than we were faced with the problems of the Republic of South Africa in the form of two small white cards, which we were required to complete. One of the questions on the card was 'Race?' I was tempted to fill in the blank space with the word 'human' (which oddly enough was not one of the three alternatives listed), but the inimical glare of a Boer policeman standing beside me and an anxiety not to be late for dinner with our hosts, whom we had neither of us met, induced me to scrub this out and write tamely: 'European'. (A couple of years before, my father Randolph Churchill had had his passport confiscated at this same airport when, offered the choice of putting his 'Signature or Mark' at the bottom of the card, he had opted for the latter alternative, covering his right thumb in ink from his ball-point pen and planting it boldly at the foot of the page.)

To explain Harry F. Oppenheimer, if that were necessary, I can do no better than to quote John Gunther in his comprehensive and most readable *Inside Africa*:

> The Anglo American Investment Trust (Oppenheimer) owns 20 per cent of the De Beers equity. De Beers (Oppenheimer) holds 92 per cent of the preferred shares of the Premier (Transvaal) Diamond Mining Company, and 96·4 per cent of the equity of Consolidated Diamond Mines of South-West Africa Ltd. The Diamond Corporation is owned by De Beers, Consolidated Diamonds and Anglo American Investment Trust. And the De Beers Investment Trust is owned in turn by the Diamond Corporation, De Beers Consolidated, Consolidated Diamonds and Anglo American. No matter which way you add it up, the answer always comes out the same—Oppenheimer.

Gunther was writing in 1953 (and since then the percentages have gone up fractionally); he was writing of the father, Sir Ernest Oppenheimer, who, born in Germany of Jewish parents, had come out to Kimberley just after the turn of the century at the age of twenty-two and made his fortune in diamonds and later in gold. When his father died, Harry Oppenheimer took over the business. And today Anglo American with more than 160 subsidiaries and associated companies accounts for 34 per cent of all South Africa's gold production or approximately 25 per cent of world production; the Central Selling Organization, administered by De Beers, markets about 80 per cent of the world's diamond production.

During our five-day stay in Johannesburg our host arranged for Arnold and myself to visit a gold mine belonging to the South African Land and Exploration Company on the East Rand. Before going down the mine we stripped and put on some overalls, boots, waterproof jackets and miners' helmets. In this rig-up we were put in a small, dark, dank cage which sped downwards into the earth at 2,500 ft per minute (without passengers it operates at 3,500 ft per min.—as fast as our aircraft in a nose-dive). The cage clattered downwards for about a minute and a half. When it stopped we were in an enormous cavern 4,000 ft below ground-level. Here was a hive of activity. The shift had just been changed: hundreds of African mineworkers were pouring out of the four-tier cages in which they had arrived from the surface. Others, who had just finished work, were waiting their turn to be hoisted up to ground-level. We climbed aboard a small rail-car behind a diesel locomotive which carried us three or four miles through a tunnel to another shaft-head where we waited with the rest of the new shift for some blasting to take place at a lower level. An exploratory tunnel was being driven in this part of the mine in the hope of cutting across a seam of ore which, from previous excavations, was believed to be there.

Suddenly the dimly-lit cavern trembled violently and we heard the muffled rumble of the detonations from the depths below. That was the signal for us to get into another cage-lift which took us to the lowest level of the mine more than 7,000 ft underground. At this depth we were well below sea-level. The heat and humidity were intense. And although two large exhaust and ventilation pipes were in operation, there was still a strong, acrid smell of cordite from the explosions. We made our way along the water-logged tunnel to the rock-face where there lay a great heap of rock and slag waiting to be cleared away by the new shift. In the gloom, pierced only by the beams of the head-lamps worn by the miners, we could see men hosing down the rubble to prevent the suffocating and injurious dust flying around. Others were operating a small machine that ran on rails; with lots of huffing and puffing (for it was pneumatically operated) it charged forward grabbing a load of blasted rock in its scoop and then ran back a few feet tossing the rock over its head into an open rail-car waiting behind it. The combination of heat and humidity was such as to make memories of the New York subway during a heat-wave, feel like a cold shower. Although we had shed the heavy waterproof jackets at the 4,000 ft level and were wearing only thin overalls, Arnold and I were sweating profusely. We did not stay down long, but for those who have to work from day to day in this oppressive atmosphere it must be a considerable physical strain.

It was a pleasant sensation to be back once more on the surface. The sun was dipping in the sky and I breathed deeply the cool and fresh evening air which so often one takes for granted. The underground manager, a South African of English origin, who had been showing us round the mine, took us to see the giant winding equipment that carries the mineworkers up and down, and brings hundreds of tons of ore from the depths of the earth each day. Thousands of feet of steel cable are wound around gigantic drums which revolve slowly at first, then building up terrific momentum, spin faster and faster until the cable is being paid out on one drum and hauled in on another at the rate of 40 m.p.h. The ore is processed in a nearby plant which we were told has an output of approximately £11,000 worth of gold ingots a day.

When I asked the underground manager if there were frequent strikes by the African workers he answered that they were so well looked after that they would not want to strike—anyway Government legislation had made it illegal for Africans to strike. Thereupon I rather naïvely enquired how the African Trade Unions reacted to this ban on strikes. 'They don't,' he replied, 'for the simple reason that African Trade Unions are illegal too.' Thus out of a work-force of 6,000 employed at this mine, it is only the 460 white miners who have the right to strike.

African labour on the Rand is almost all migrant. Most of the miners sign on for an eighteen-month contract. This is radically different from the policy pursued by the Belgians in the Congo where a serious and successful effort was made to stabilize the labour force by offering promotion to skilled Africans and by encouraging them to bring their families, for whom housing, schools and hospitals were provided. In South Africa things are otherwise. The Industrial Conciliation Act (1956) imposes an industrial colour-bar, reserving most of the more responsible and better paid jobs for whites only, leaving the African little opportunity of bettering his lot. The large mining corporations, particularly Oppenheimer's Anglo American, have for many years wanted to stabilize at least a proportion of the African labour force. Increasing mechanization in the mines, especially in the new and prodigiously rich Orange Free State goldfields, has created an ever-growing demand for skilled and semi-skilled African labour. Skilled Africans operating with modern equipment would have a far higher production quota than the present untrained armies of migrant mineworkers. This would enable the conditions of work and the standard of living of the African mineworker to be immeasurably improved, bringing their wages into line with the European miners, whose labour at the moment commands an enormous price differential.

But all attempts by Oppenheimer to implement this scheme, which would benefit both the African workers and the mining companies, have been consistently frustrated by Dr Verwoerd's Nationalist Government. The following is an extract from a report published recently by the Anglo American Corporation:

As the Orange Free State mines are more highly mechanized than the older gold mines on the Witwatersrand, the need has increased for responsible Natives capable of acting as super-

visors and of handling mechanical equipment. These positions
are filled, where possible, with settled married workers living
with their families in the Native married quarters (or villages)
attached to the mines. The scheme is restricted by Government
direction to Union Natives who belong to the category of
essential and semi-skilled workers, and to *not more than three
per cent* (my italics) of the total labour force of a mine.

Thus the 'stubborn and mulish ignorance of the Boers' (to
borrow one of Lord Randolph's favourite epithets) not only
denies the African any chance of political and social advancement,
but even denies him the possibility of improving his lot by his
own skill and hard work. Such injustice cannot fail to arouse the
resentment of the African population and the disgust of outsiders.

For the duration of his contract the African mineworker is
housed in a compound near the mine: he is not allowed to bring
his family with him. Unfortunately Arnold and I did not have
the time to see the compound of the mine we visited, but the
underground manager assured us that the living conditions,
medical care and food of the African miners were all a great deal
better than they would get in their own homes. He added that they
all put on weight during their time at the mine. Doubtless they
are well cared for. However I could not help feeling that to
someone who has lived his life in the seclusion and happiness of
a small African village with its round mud huts ringing with
laughter, and who has been free to wander through the jungle or
roam across the plain close to the wonders and beauty of Nature,
life in the mines must be a misery. On the Rand scenery is dull;
the horizon is broken only by giant mountains of slag and the
winding gear of the pits. There is little freedom and the work
is strenuous. At the pithead we saw some of the new mining
recruits squatting on the ground being given instruction in

underground safety by an African miner. Their faces betrayed a dejection and resignation we saw nowhere else on the continent. The African's greatest quality is his gaiety and light-heartedness, which in West Africa is effusive, in East Africa somewhat subdued, but in South Africa, so far as I could judge from a brief visit, almost entirely suppressed. It is only in South Africa that one can see what Livingstone meant when he wrote: 'The strangest disease I have seen in this country seems really to be broken-heartedness.' Nevertheless it is a remarkable fact that a great proportion of African labour on the Rand comes from outside South Africa—mostly from Nyasaland and Mozambique. And although it is a criminal offence for African mineworkers to absent themselves from work, leave their jobs or go on strike, there is no question of forced labour. Africans come to the Rand of their own free will or rather, of economic necessity. When their contracts are up most of them return to their villages and, with the money they have earned, buy themselves a wife or two. They regard a spell in the mines as a challenge—which it certainly is.

*   *   *

Thirty miles north of Johannesburg lies South Africa's administrative capital, Pretoria. It was here, in a drab single-storey building known as the State Model Schools (which we visited and found still in use today) that my grandfather Winston Churchill had been imprisoned by the Boers in 1899; his subsequent dramatic escape proved to be a turning-point in his career. At the time he was not yet twenty-five years old, but he had already seen as much of the world as most people see in a lifetime. He had heard his first shot fired in anger on 30 November 1895—his twenty-first birthday—in Cuba where he had gone to observe the Cuban Revolutionary War against Spain. He had campaigned on the Indian frontier with Sir Bindon Blood's Malakand Field Force. And he had charged with the 21st Lancers at Omdurman. His one ambition was to get into politics. But in those days, since there was no pay, it needed money to become a Member of Parliament. His father, Lord Randolph, had died early in 1895. The 5,000 Rand Mine shares that he had purchased at par value at the time of his visit to South Africa in 1891, had risen to nearly twenty times their original value by the time of his death. Their spectacular rise continued and had Lord Randolph lived another year he would have had a considerable fortune. As it was, when he died, his assets barely balanced his debts and the shares had to be sold. From then on, until he was forty-five years old, when he inherited some money from a distant relation, my grandfather was entirely dependent upon his sense of adventure and his pen for his livelihood. He therefore resigned his army commission, which he could not afford, and proceeded to write an account of the campaign in the Sudan, entitled *The River War*, which earned him some much needed money. He then fought a by-election at Oldham in Lancashire, but failed to get in. However, in 1899 the Boer War broke out and he went to South Africa as a correspondent for the *Morning Post*. Little more than two weeks after his arrival in Cape Town he was on board an armoured train in Natal which was derailed and attacked by the Boers. He made his way to the engine which was still on the rails. As he reached it a shrapnel shell burst overhead wounding the engine-driver who was the only person capable of operating the train. My grandfather encouraged, entreated, cajoled and, it seems, even promised the man a medal before he could persuade the driver to return to his post. (This he had no authority whatever to do. Nevertheless, when he became Home Secretary ten years later, he kept his promise and the engine-driver was awarded the Albert Medal, the highest civilian award.)

For more than an hour under a constant hail of bullets and shrapnel he stood in the open, giving orders to the engine-driver, in an attempt to extricate the engine and tender from the wreckage. He eventually succeeded and the engine managed to get away laden with all the wounded. A few minutes later he was captured by a man who was to become a great friend of his in later life—Louis Botha who in 1906 was elected the first Prime Minister of the Transvaal. Then, with the other prisoners from the armoured train, he was taken under guard to Pretoria and imprisoned in the State Model Schools.

It did not take him long to discover that prison life did not agree with him. And within a few days he had evolved a plan of fantastic audacity. It was no ordinary plan of escape: it was a plan for bringing the war to a speedy, victorious and virtually bloodless conclusion. First the sixty British officers imprisoned in the State Model Schools would, in the middle of the night, overpower their ten-man guard and seize their weapons. Second, they would head for the Pretoria race-course where more than 2,000 British soldiers were confined inside a barbed-wire enclosure. There they would overwhelm the guard and release the prisoners. The third step was to seize from within the fortified town of Pretoria, in which there were no more than 500 people capable of bearing arms, since almost every able-bodied man was at the front. If these three steps could be achieved, dawn would find a not insubstantial British force in possession of the enemy capital, with sufficient arms, ammunition and food to hold out for a long defence. In *My Early Life* he concludes: 'If we got Pretoria we could hold it for months. And what a feat of arms! President Kruger and his government would be prisoners in our hands. He had talked of "staggering humanity". But here indeed was something to stagger him.'

This was certainly a plan of escape on a grandiose scale. Who can say that it might not have succeeded? Surprise is a potent weapon. As it was, the two or three senior officers among the prisoners thought the scheme too bold and pronounced against it. The project had to be abandoned. Thereafter he had to plan his escape on a more modest scale. Nevertheless within a month of his capture by the Boers, the young war correspondent was once again at large, having one night climbed out of a latrine window and scrambled over a wall no more than fifteen yards away from two sentries, standing with their backs turned. He made his way to the railway line and jumped on the first east-bound freight train that passed. Ten days later he reached Lourenço Marques, capital of the Portuguese colony of Mozambique. He was once more a free man, more than this—he was a hero.

The British public had just read glowing accounts in their newspapers of his exploits in the armoured train incident and many people had suggested that he ought to be given the Victoria Cross. (This was impossible since he was at the time a civilian. Had he still been in the Army it seems likely that he would have been awarded this, the highest honour for gallantry in the field of battle.) News of his escape came at the end of a week which had seen several serious military reverses for the British and as a result it received universal acclaim. Suddenly he was world-famous. Thirty years later, writing *My Early Life*, he looked back on his capture:

This misfortune, could I have foreseen the future, was to lay the foundations of my later life. I was not to be done out of the campaign. I was not to languish as a prisoner. I was to escape, and by escaping was to gain a public reputation or notoriety which made me well-known henceforward among my country-men, and made me acceptable as a candidate in a great many constituencies. I was also put in the position to earn the money which for many years assured my independence and the means of entering Parliament.

In the Khaki Election of the following year (1900) he succeeded in winning Oldham—by 230 votes—and entered upon his Parliamentary career.

*   *   *

Basutoland is a country of mountains and swiftly-flowing rivers, of vivid green hillsides and magnificent waterfalls. The Basuto people came into being during the early nineteenth century as a combination of tribes which, to resist the depredations of the warlike Zulus, had united under a chief named Moshesh and retired to the Drakensberg Mountains. In 1868 Moshesh, who had ruled the Basuto for nearly fifty years, sought British protection. This was granted, and in the last two years of his life the aged chief conducted a correspondence with Queen Victoria. Today Basutoland is still a British Protectorate or, more properly, a High Commission Territory which, together with Swaziland and Bechuanaland, is administered directly from London. Geographically and economically Basutoland, and to a lesser extent the other two territories, are part of South Africa; indeed Basutoland is completely encircled by the Republic which has long claimed that these British-protected enclaves should form part of South Africa. On the face of it this seems a sensible idea; and it would have been carried into effect long ago by the British Government were it not for the distasteful racial policies of the Boers. The position of these territories has become more precarious than ever since 1961 when South Africa became a Republic and, under pressure, quit the Commonwealth. The fact that more than two-thirds of Basutoland's young men go at some time or another to work in the Rand Mines has led to the country's political awakening. In 1959 the Basutoland Congress Party won the elections held under a new constitution and there is now a growing demand for independence. It seems most unlikely that the South African Government in its present frame of mind would lightly accept the existence of an independent African state within her borders, particularly since Basutoland is already regarded both as a haven of refuge for African nationalists and as a base for subversive activities in southern Africa. The very existence of Basutoland is dependent on the maintenance of good relations with the Republic; and it is difficult to see how these can continue once British protection is withdrawn.

The Paramount Chief of the Basutos, Constantine Bereng Seeiso, a young man in his mid-twenties, had been a friend of Arnold's at Oxford. However, before he had completed his three years at the University he had been obliged to return to Basutoland in a hurry in order to push his step-mother, Amelia 'Mantsebo Seeiso, off the throne which she had assumed in his absence. Arnold and I rented a Land Rover in the tiny capital of Maseru and from there drove across Basutoland's rolling foothills on a rough track to the village of Matsieng where we called on the young Paramount Chief. He was at his desk in a long single-storied building made of wood; a large photograph of Queen Elizabeth II hung on the wall behind him. He told us that Basutoland had been self-governing since 1959 and was now ready for independence, although he did not make it clear how he was going to handle the vexed question of his country's relations with South Africa.

During our brief stay in Basutoland we were involved in a road accident. We had one morning flown up into the mountains (some of which are over 11,000 ft high) to see a few of the more spectacular waterfalls, and on our return to Maseru airfield a European offered to give us a lift into the town in his car. I wrote in my diary at the time:

Arnold and I could see it coming a mile away; this fellow never hooted or slowed up when a child started walking across the middle of the road; he did not even swerve or brake but ran straight into the child (he was, it appears, very short-sighted). A big crowd gathered round and it took some time to find the mother, whom we drove with the child to the Queen Elizabeth Hospital. As it was the lunch-hour, no doctors could be found in the hospital. The child had a couple of wounds on his head and I thought there was a possibility that it had a fractured skull. The driver, with little tact and even less sympathy, told the mother: 'It's amazing more of these little nippers don't get run over.' He seemed remarkably unconcerned by the whole thing. The African nurses were scarcely any more helpful, saying that it was impossible to disturb the doctors during lunch. I was of a rather different opinion and with great difficulty we managed to get a doctor to leave his lunch to come and attend to the child.

*   *   *

We reached Cape Town two and a half months after leaving England—hardly a record for the London to Cape Town route which has been a challenge to pilots of light aircraft since the 1920's. Many made the flight successfully: others were never heard of again. One famous flight was that of Captain Lancaster— it was thirty years before his aircraft and his remains were found in the heart of the Sahara. Today, with more reliable machines

Johannesburg: von Bohlen 7,000 ft below ground-level
AND *Angola: author in Luanda*

and an increasing number of radio-navigational aids, the flight is by no means as hazardous as it was in the old days, although it is far from uneventful or unexciting.

Cape Town is perhaps the most attractive city in Africa. It stands on the sea near the point where the Indian Ocean and South Atlantic meet, with Table Mountain rising up steeply behind it. The climate is that of the Mediterranean; vineyards and plants of every kind flourish. The city was founded in 1652, and many lovely old Dutch buildings remain. But Cape Town has moved with the times and today it boasts a battery of skyscrapers and a thriving port. And nowhere else on the continent did we drive on a six-lane highway. At times one almost forgets one is in Africa.

The night before we headed north on our return journey to England, our host and hostess gave a barbecue party beside the swimming-pool of their beautiful old Dutch house in the hills above Cape Town. I soon found myself engaged in a discussion on politics with one of the other guests—an elderly Boer. I had heard him shouting: 'It'll be fifty years before these people learn to pull a lavatory chain!' I therefore ventured to ask him how long he thought the whites in South Africa could maintain their supremacy. This elicited the reply: 'Before we surrender we'll kill every bloody nigger in the place, and you bloody liberals (pointing at Arnold and myself, presumably taking us for South Africans) will be the first to get shot.' At this juncture, I think Arnold and I (standing beside the pool) were perhaps unable to restrain a laugh: anyway the next minute saw the pair of us sailing through the air towards the swimming-pool— fortunately we were able to bring our fellow-guest with us into the water.

In *London to Ladysmith via Pretoria* my grandfather records a conversation he had with a Boer soon after he had been taken

Angola: jungle patrol with Portuguese army

prisoner in 1899. He asked the Boer why his people were so opposed to British rule. The following was the reply:

> *We* know how to treat Kaffirs in *this* country. Fancy letting the black filth walk on the pavement! Educate a Kaffir! Ah, that's you English all over. We educate 'em with a stick. Treat 'em with humanity and consideration—I like that. They were put here by the God Almighty to work for us. We'll stand no damned nonsense from them. We'll keep them in their proper places. What do you think? Insist on their proper treatment will you? Ah, that's what we're going to see about now. We'll settle whether you English are to interfere with us before this war is over.

My grandfather concludes:

> What is the true and original root of Dutch aversion to British rule? It is not Slagters Nek, nor Broomplatz, nor Majuba, nor the Jameson Raid. It is the abiding fear and hatred of the movement that seeks to place the native on a level with the white man.

This then is the crux of the matter. The Boer regards the African as no better than an animal and dislikes the British for fear of being made to treat the African like a human being. This was the argument between Briton and Boer at the time of the Boer War, and this is the argument that continues today. Unfortunately for the Africans and for the more civilized Europeans, 60 per cent of the white (or voting) population is Boer, and from a comparison of the conversation my grandfather had with his Boer and the one I had beside the swimming-pool with my Boer, it is clear that Boer opinion has advanced little since the nineteenth century. Boer thinking is firmly entrenched behind the dogmatic beliefs of the Dutch Reformed Church with a bigotry the like of which there has been nothing since the days of the Inquisition in Catholic Spain. Dr Hendrik Verwoerd, a firm believer in the Divine Right of White Men, declared on being elected Prime Minister in April 1958: 'I believe the will of God was revealed in the ballot.' I should hasten to add that by no means every Boer is an ignorant, narrow-minded, self-righteous bigot. There are of course many who are civilized and well-informed, and whose outlook is more reasonable and rational. It would also be a mistake to suppose that every Briton in South Africa is a lily-white liberal; nothing could be further from the truth. However it is a plain fact that both the Government and the electorate that put it in power are predominantly Boer in complexion and it is they who must bear the ultimate responsibility for South Africa's distasteful racial policies.

The position of South Africa is radically different from that of any other country in Africa. In Kenya for instance, where the ratio of African to European is more than 100 to 1, it is clear that the European was in no position to resist the demands of African Nationalism. Besides this, Kenya's European population amounted to little more than 60,000, few of whom have been there more than two generations. Should it ever prove necessary, it would not be an impossible task to repatriate these people or for them to find homes elsewhere, possibly in Canada or Australia. The same is true to a lesser degree of Southern Rhodesia where the European population of 220,000 is outnumbered by 16 to 1. But in South Africa, where there are more than five times as many Europeans as in all the rest of Africa put together and the ratio of black to white is only 4 to 1, the situation is very different. It would be virtually impossible to find homes for South Africa's 3,250,000 Europeans, some of whose families have been living there for more than three centuries. Some solution has to be arrived at whereby the European population can remain—and remain without having to live under the tyranny of a black Verwoerd. For unless a solution acceptable to African and European can be found the future of South Africa is grim.

Unlike many who have visited South Africa—and many more who have not—I can see no clear and easy solution to her problems. African Nationalists, left-wing Liberals, Socialists and Communists demand an African Government on the basis of one man one vote. This could never be a peaceable solution. If Greek and Turk cannot live side by side in peace on the tiny island of Cyprus, how much less likely it is that African and European could do so in South Africa, where racial tension and fear are incomparably greater. It is most unlikely that any African government could restrain its supporters from repaying with interest the injustice they have suffered at the hands of the Boers. For this reason it is inconceivable that South Africa's Europeans would ever submit to African rule without a fight.

It seems there are only two peaceful solutions possible: Multi-racial government or partition. A multi-racial government based on a universal adult franchise subject to an educational qualification, would in many ways be the most desirable solution. It could only work if a strong constitution could be framed that would safeguard the African population while the Europeans still had the greater share of the votes, and protect the Europeans once majority control had passed to the Africans. To work such a constitution would require great tact and restraint by both sides, and it is unlikely that this could ever be achieved, considering the forces at work in Africa today. It is doubtful that either side would be prepared even to consider such a radical compromise of their stated views in the first place.

Partition is perhaps the more hopeful solution. The South African Government taking the doctrine of 'apartheid', or 'separate development' as it is now more primly called, towards its logical conclusion has begun to set up 'Bantustans', territories in the less developed areas of South Africa where local administration is to be in African hands. A step in this direction was taken in November 1963 when elections were held in the Transkei, the first of the Bantustans so far established. Dr Verwoerd's Bantustans might one day form a basis for partition, but the difficulties of such a policy are innumerable. The European is dependent on African labour: the African is dependent upon a thriving industry for employment. The South African economy is one entity. Theoretically it might be possible for two South African states, one African and one European, to share in the running of an integrated economy. But in practice it is more likely that there would be acrimony over how the land, the gold, the diamonds etc. are to be divided. Nor is there any prospect that such a solution would in any way appease the African Nationalists who demand that the map of Africa be painted black all over.

If, however, neither side is prepared to compromise—and there is little sign of it at the moment—it is difficult to see how a grisly explosion in South Africa can be avoided. There can be little doubt that if it came to a show-down the Europeans could 'kill every bloody nigger in the place' as some Boers threaten to do. There are only four Africans to every European, and the guns and aircraft are in the hands of Europeans. It would seem that only outside intervention could topple the South African Government. Nor could this be done by any forces that the Afro-Asian nations might put in the field. South Africa is a rich country and although she has only 6 per cent of the total population of the African continent she accounts for 40 per cent of Africa's industrial production. She has a strong, well-equipped army as well as a substantial air force. The Boers are fierce and fearless fighters—as the British learned to their cost at the time of the Boer War when it took them two and a half years, £220 million and about 450,000 troops to bring 87,000 Boers to heel. If, however, the Afro-Asian nations were able to secure the intervention of one or other of the Great Powers, as they succeeded in doing in the Congo, the situation in southern Africa would be transformed overnight. And it must be remembered that by playing off the Soviet Union and the United States against each other, the smaller nations are able to wield power and resources infinitely greater than their own—provided, of course, that one of the Great Powers is prepared to let itself be pulled about by the tail.

XI

JUNGLE PATROL

T<small>HE SKY WAS</small> grey and a misty drizzle was falling as we took off from Cape Town. We turned the Comanche on to a northerly heading and soon Table Mountain, shrouded in a bank of low cloud, disappeared into the mists. Once the Cape was behind us the clouds began to scatter, enabling us to climb to 11,000 ft. And as we reached the fringe of the Kalahari Desert the last wispy trace of cloud vanished. Nearly 800 miles of desert separates Cape Town from Windhoek, the capital of South-West Africa. This was our longest flight so far. The Comanche's safe range since we had no extra fuel tanks was only 600 miles at its normal cruising speed of 180 m.p.h. However by lowering our cruising speed to 160 m.p.h. and thereby cutting the fuel consumption from 12 to 8·5 gallons per hour, we would be able to reach Windhoek with half an hour's reserve fuel. We therefore reduced power as soon as we levelled off at our cruising altitude. Here we not only had a greater range, but the flight would be both safer and more comfortable.

To be flying a light aircraft more than two miles high over a burning desert is one of the most exhilarating feelings in the world. The clarity of the moistureless air is intense. At this altitude the horizon extends more than a hundred miles on all sides and the desert stretches out below as far as the eye can see. The glare of the noon-day sun strikes fiercely upwards from the barren waste, yet here the air is cool and fresh. One has the sensation of being on top of the world—provided of course that the engine continues to purr smoothly and you know where you are. After coming so close to disaster over the jungles of Central Africa I had determined to pay particular attention to my navigation whenever we were over featureless country. I therefore made a habit of establishing our position every ten minutes. After marking where we were on the map, I would try to find another landmark about thirty miles ahead and compute the time we should pass over it to the nearest half-minute. In this way I found it possible to make use of relatively insignificant landmarks such as a dried-up water-course or an outcrop of rocks which one could not hope to recognize unless one kept a very exact check on one's position. Flying in Europe or the United States it is relatively difficult to miss such obvious landmarks as towns, roads and railways. In Africa it is very different and much more precision is necessary in navigation.

Unlike the great yellow sand-seas of the Sahara, the Kalahari is predominantly red and rocky. Dark conical hills protrude from its flattish surface and in places there are deep canyons reminiscent of parts of Colorado. As we drew nearer to Windhoek which stands at 5,500 ft among some craggy mountains, we noticed here and there small, isolated cattle-farms beneath us, although from the air we could see little sign of vegetation. South-West Africa has a population of less than two inhabitants per square mile and it must be a hardy existence eking a livelihood out of land so barren.

Windhoek is the chief centre of trade for ranchers hundreds of miles around. It has a pronounced German influence remaining from the days when it was the capital of German South-West Africa. Many of the houses have high, steeply sloping roofs obviously designed to allow the snow to slide off, but looking rather quaint on the edge of the Kalahari. Set on the side of a hill overlooking the town there are even a couple of miniature *schlosses*, such as one might find on the banks of the Rhine. German is still the principal language, followed by Afrikaans and English, although it has been under South African mandate since 1919. In spite of the claim of the ranchers that their country is the 'Texas of Africa', the chief wealth of South-West Africa comes not from its cattle but from its diamonds on the coast of Namaqualand.

The diamond-fields belong to one of Oppenheimer's Anglo American Group of companies and are thought to be the richest in the world. Since the diamonds here are largely alluvial and one is liable to stub one's toe against them while taking a stroll along the beach, rigorous security precautions are taken and the coast is patrolled by the South African Navy and Air Force. One of the South-Westers we met during our overnight stay in Windhoek told us that he had some shares in a company that was about to begin mining operations the following week for diamonds on the sea-bed, using suction-dredging equipment to bring the diamonds to the surface. He was most excited by the project.

Windhoek has some of the worst slums in the whole of Africa. Near the edge of the town there is the most appalling shanty-village where the native Africans live in huts made of scrap-metal and cardboard. Some have been re-housed in a newly-built village, which we drove up to but could not visit as it had just turned 6 p.m. and thereafter it is illegal for Europeans to be in the African district and vice versa. It is unfortunate that South Africa

appropriates to herself the greater part of South-West Africa's
balance of trade surplus, instead of applying it to the welfare of
the Africans. Certain African countries have raised the question
of South-West Africa in the United Nations and in the International Court of Justice at the Hague, in the hope of having the
mandate revoked from South Africa. It is doubtful that the
Republic would even consider surrendering South-West Africa
which she has ruled for nearly half a century; indeed the Nationalist Government has on several occasions declared its intention
of annexing the territory.

*   *   *

To the traveller arriving hot-foot from South Africa, Angola
presents a staggering contrast. This is particularly striking to a
layman on African affairs who has seen Portugal and South
Africa put daily in the same pillory by the world press and
assumes they are all the same kettle of fish. Coming from the land
of apartheid our surprise can be imagined when, on the night of
our arrival in Angola's capital, Luanda, we went to dine at the
best hotel and found an African man and a European woman
dining together at the next table. It was no less astonishing
the next morning to see children—black, white and coffee-
coloured—shouting and playing together as they came out of
the schools at midday. This is a far cry from South Africa, and
it is soon evident to the visitor that there is no visible sign of a
colour-bar or racial discrimination in Angola.

A Portuguese official made the point when he told us how not
long before, a large party of American journalists had arrived in
Luanda and had asked him how many blacks, whites and mulattoes went to school in Angola. He explained: 'I told them how

many children we have in our schools, but we don't count them by race as they seem to do in America—as far as we are concerned they are just children.' The easy-going manner of the Portuguese makes them better suited in many ways to understand and appreciate the light-hearted temperament of the African, than does the cold, more authoritarian manner of the Briton or the Boer. They have fewer inhibitions than the more nordic Europeans and this enables them to mix more freely with the Africans. A Portuguese told me: 'The Dutch, French and, even on occasion, you British have taken African women as mistresses—we have taken them for our wives. God created the white man and the black man, but it was the Portuguese who created the mulatto.'

The Portuguese Government in Lisbon regards the African territories of Angola, Mozambique and Portuguese Guinea as provinces of Portugal. The inhabitants of these overseas possessions are regarded as Portuguese citizens and they enjoy all the rights of Portuguese citizenship (however few these may be). To differentiate between the metropolitan Portuguese and the Portuguese of Angola, many of whom have been there since long before the Pilgrim Fathers reached America, it is convenient to call the latter Angolese. Several of the Angolese we talked to complained: 'Why won't Portugal give us our independence as she gave it to Brazil in 1822?' Adding in a whisper, so as not to be overheard by the state security police (Policia Internacional e de Defesa de Estado): 'We have no great love for Dr Salazar.' It would seem that a proportion at least of the European population of Angola favours independence from Portugal. Later on our journey when we reached Ghana, we heard that Dr Nkrumah had not long before received an Angolan nationalist delegation at Accra Airport—to his dismay half of them were white men. But the Portuguese Government is determined to maintain its hold on its African colonies, whose economies are closely integrated with that of Portugal. Angola alone is fourteen times the size of Portugal and is rich in sugar, coffee, palm oil, petroleum and diamonds. Portugal is not a wealthy country; without her colonial empire she would become even poorer. It is therefore highly unlikely that she would ever of her own free will grant Angola independence, under either a black or a white government. If any people can build a multi-racial society in Africa it is the Portuguese who stand the best chance of doing so. Their achievement in Brazil, a country almost the size of the United States, has been remarkable. But whether a similar society can be evolved today in Africa under the direction of a European power, remains a highly dubious proposition.

Neither Arnold nor I knew anyone in Angola; we therefore paid a visit on the head of the National Tourist Office. He asked us what we would like to see. I told him we wanted to have a look at Luanda, visit the countryside in the vicinity of the capital and then go on a patrol with the Portuguese Army in the northern part of Angola where the trouble is. To my surprise, he said he would be delighted to arrange for us to do just that.

Luanda is a city of great beauty. It stands on the cool glittering waters of the South Atlantic where a palm-studded sand-bar juts out into the ocean, forming a lagoon and a natural harbour. Dominating the scene is the fortress of San Miguel which dates back to the sixteenth century, a reminder that it was the Portuguese who were the pioneers of European exploration along the coasts of Africa. It is now nearly 500 years since the first Portuguese reached Angola in 1482—even before Columbus had discovered America. Luanda is full of charm and gaiety. It boasts many excellent restaurants, which serve what are perhaps the best lobsters in the world, and there are numerous night-clubs where African and European mix without any of the formality so evident in other parts of colonial Africa. One of the most remarkable sights, and something we did not find even in the newly-independent countries, is to see Europeans in shops and offices working in a subordinate capacity to Africans. Along Luanda's sea-front were several large buildings nearing completion—new hotels, new schools and new government buildings—a sure sign of Portuguese confidence in their ability to remain in Angola.

Arrangements had been made for Arnold and myself to visit a sugar plantation about forty miles outside of Luanda, and a former journalist who had been born and brought up in Angola came with us as our guide. The plantation, which was owned by a Portuguese company based in Lisbon, was extensive and employed some 4,000 men. We drove up long avenues of palm-trees which bordered the fields where the sugar-cane was growing. We were then shown a settlement of white-washed concrete houses, to which the workers were returning after a day in the fields. Nearby was a row of better-built houses which we assumed were for the European staff. We were mistaken; and although one or two belonged to Europeans, the majority were inhabited by Africans and mulattoes holding responsible positions on the plantation. The houses, although small, were attractively furnished. There were flowers on the tables and several houses had radios. Standing in the middle of the living-room of one of the houses we saw a large, bright red motor-cycle, of which its African owner was inordinately proud. 'Give us time,' said the Portuguese manager, 'and all our employees will have houses like these.' Next, we were taken to see the plantation's hospital. I have never seen such a spotlessly clean hospital in all my life. The walls of the rooms and the passages were covered in white tiling and the operating-theatre seemed to have all the most modern equipment. In an inner courtyard, which had been made into a garden, several of the patients were sitting in their long white hospital-clothes taking the evening sun. The Portuguese doctor told us that half the hospital's 120 beds were in use. He was the only European doctor there; the rest of his staff were African. It was obvious that the Portuguese were only showing us what they wanted us to see, and they were evidently particularly proud of this hospital. Nevertheless the mere fact that it existed was remarkable.

From Luanda we were able to obtain special clearance to fly to the provincial town of Carmona in the north where large numbers of the 40,000 Portuguese troops in Angola were in action. It is extremely difficult to get a balanced view of what happened at the time of the uprising against the Portuguese in March 1961. This is in part due to the fact that many commentators on African affairs have allowed themselves to become violently partisan supporters either of Colonialism or African Nationalism, with a consequent distortion of the truth in their reports. Thus the accounts emanating from the rebel headquarters in Leopoldville, capital of the ex-Belgian Congo, and from Portuguese sources in Angola, are entirely contradictory. The rebels claim that the uprising was spontaneous and that it was set off by Portuguese brutality to labourers on a plantation near San Salvador do Congo sixty miles from the Congo border. They assert that the revolt had the popular support of all the African population throughout Angola. The Portuguese on the other hand contend that the uprising was engineered by a terrorist organization based in the Congo and financed by Peking and Moscow, which had no widespread support from the Africans of Angola. They cite as evidence the fact that the trouble was confined almost entirely to the northern part of the country which borders on the Congo and they point out that in March 1961 in all of Angola there were no more than 2,000 Portuguese soldiers and 700 police, half of whom were African. This being so, the Portuguese ask, how was it possible that the revolt did not spread to other parts of the country or affect so much as 5 per cent of Angola's 4 million Africans? However this may be, there is no doubt that the terrorists indulged in an orgy of butchery that was directed not only against the Portuguese settlers in their isolated farmhouses, but also against Africans who remained in their villages and refused to join in the slaughter. In the three weeks that followed 15 March 1961, 1,300 Europeans and a far larger number of Africans were killed by the terrorists, who were in the habit of mutilating their victims' bodies in the most appalling way. There is also little doubt that the Portuguese settlers when the opportunity presented itself retaliated with the utmost brutality. In the event, either from fear of terrorist attacks on their villages or of reprisals by the Portuguese or perhaps both, an estimated 260,000 Africans fled into the jungle and many of them made their way to the Congo.

As soon as the news of the uprising reached Lisbon reinforcements were sent to Angola and a large-scale military build-up began. The Portuguese Army soon re-established control of the towns in the northern provinces and of the major lines of communication. Nevertheless, terrorist activity has continued in the area which, with its dense jungle and tall elephant-grass, is ideally suited to guerilla warfare.

Arnold and I arrived in Carmona armed with a letter of introduction to the District Governor who arranged for us to go on a jungle patrol that was setting out at dawn the next day from N'Gage, a small village a couple of hours' drive to the southeast. We travelled to N'Gage that night with a Portuguese Army convoy and reached the village soon after midnight. Here the local administrative officer kindly put us up for the night in his house. One of the chief tasks of the Portuguese Army besides maintaining order, has been to regain the confidence of the villagers. Posters had been stuck up in the villages or nailed to trees by the wayside in an attempt to persuade the Africans, who had fled to the jungle, to return to their villages. The Portuguese claim that approximately 160,000 have already done so. Our host explained that it was his job to rehabilitate the local population and to bring life in the villages back to normal. Schools had been burnt and crops destroyed, and it was necessary to reconstitute the local administration and relieve hardship.

The next morning we were up at dawn, rigged up in camouflage jackets and double-peaked caps which had been loaned us by the Portuguese. The patrol, consisting of about twenty men in one Land Rover and two jeeps, drew up outside the administrative officer's house. I was surprised to see that one of the soldiers, a corporal, was African. Our host told us that there were many Africans serving with the Portuguese Army. Most of them, he said, come from tribes in the south of Angola and were formidable fighters. After weapons and ammunition had been distributed—Arnold stuffed a couple of hand-grenades into his pocket—we set out into the jungle. The following is an account I recorded in my diary at the time:

> We drove on a narrow, winding track through the dense jungle which in places had been cut back forty or fifty yards from the road to make it more difficult for the terrorists to lay ambushes. In places where the jungle gave way to savannah, elephant-grass more than five feet high was growing in the middle of the track, making it impossible to see the leading jeep only thirty feet in front of us. Elsewhere the jeep got up to its axles in mud and twice had to be pushed out by the Land Rover.
>
> This country is ideally suited to terrorism. There is nothing easier than to fell a tree across the track, lob a hand-grenade into the first vehicle that comes along, fire a burst or two from

a machine-gun and run off into the jungle. Ambushes and attacks on lonely farm-houses are the tactics favoured by the terrorists.

We visited several of these farm-houses. The most remote was on the very edge of the virgin forest. It was a long low white-washed building surrounded by coils of barbed-wire, above which were strung electric lights and beyond which the bush had been cleared back fifteen or twenty feet so as to give the inhabitants a good arc of fire. The owner, a middle-aged Portuguese woman who was alone in the house except for a young African boy, showed us the building next door which she had used to clean the coffee beans she grew on the farm. It had been set on fire by the terrorists and was completely gutted. In her house itself there were no more than two or three window-panes that had not had a bullet through them.

In the course of the morning we must have seen half a dozen farm-houses in a similar state of defence. At night, when the attacks usually come, a diesel motor is switched on in order to provide current for the lighting of the whole area, and the family takes it in turn to wait up on guard. Initially when the groups of terrorists had been large, sometimes numbering over a hundred (but often only a handful with fire-arms) farmers in an area would gather together into one house at night for greater security. Nowadays however the groups are smaller although better armed, and attacks are much less frequent.

The terrorist organization, or the 'Angolan Liberation Army' as it prefers to be known, had reached an estimated strength of 7,500 men by early 1964. The terrorists, many of whom are not even from Angola, undergo an eight-week basic training course at Camp Kinkuzu in the Congo before infiltrating into the jungles of northern Angola. Algeria has supplied them with modern weapons and in addition has provided officers well grounded in the art of terrorism from Algeria's seven-year war with France to train new recruits for Holden Roberto's Liberation Army. The Organization for African Unity established at Addis Ababa in May 1963 has so far contributed more than £170,000, but it cannot be doubted that Moscow and, since Premier Chou-En-lai's recent 'Goodwill' excursion to Africa, Peking have made their donations to such a worthy cause as the removal of Western influence from Africa by means of subversion.

The Portuguese have found it impossible to seal Angola's 1,000 mile northern frontier which is intersected by a mass of rivers and covered for the most part by dense tropical forest. The war is one of ambush and counter-ambush in the darkness of the jungle and the Portuguese, although superior in the number and quality of their soldiers, are at a disadvantage in not knowing when or where the enemy will strike next, nor are they able to strike back decisively. There is every prospect that the war in Angola, like the one carried on by Britain against Communist terrorists in the jungles of Malaya, will be a long drawn out affair. Unless the African population of Angola as a whole backs the terrorists—and there is little sign of it at the moment—or there is a large-scale revolt in Mozambique or Portuguese Guinea, which is more likely, the Portuguese Army should have no trouble holding its ground in northern Angola.

The 1961 uprising came as a profound shock to the Portuguese and, despite Dr Salazar's protestations to the contrary, it has evidently had a salutary effect on the reforming zeal of the Portuguese Government. Greater autonomy has been granted to Portugal's 'Overseas Provinces', the large plantation companies are now only allowed to take a proportion of their profits out of Angola, foreign investment has been encouraged, a university has been established at Luanda and there has been increased Government spending on education and health facilities. Angola's greatest handicap has long been the Portuguese Government which is both poor and authoritarian—an unfortunate combination. As recently as the 1950 census Portugal herself had an illiteracy rate of 30 per cent. It is not therefore surprising that in Angola it was over 90 per cent. Even today education, although free, is only compulsory from the age of seven to ten. Unlike Britain's former colonies in East and Central Africa where liberal policies were forced on the settlers by the British Government, liberalization in Portugal's colonies has, if anything, been held back by the home government. Only in the last decade has forced labour in Angola gradually been done away with. Now however Dr Salazar has been pressing ahead with long-overdue reforms. Today every inhabitant of Portugal's Overseas Provinces is a Portuguese citizen, literacy is the sole qualification for a vote, and education is compulsory. Had the colonial powers of Europe been able to look into the future fifty years ago, this might indeed have been the policy they would have chosen. As it was, not even the Portuguese began to implement this policy until 1961 and even now practice is far removed from theory, for a vote in Salazar's Portugal is worth little.

Without outside intervention Angola might well have become a peaceful and prosperous multi-racial state, a Brazil in Africa. But this was not to be. Intervention has come from Lisbon and from Algiers, backed by the Afro-Asian nations, sponsored by Moscow and Peking, and viewed not unfavourably by Washington. With this formidable array of enemies, the embryo multi-racial state of Angola seems to have little chance of survival. The total Portuguese budget amounts to only £150 million. On these meagre resources it seems doubtful that Portugal will be able to maintain indefinitely an army of over 40,000 men, 5,000 miles from Lisbon. Besides this there is the likelihood of uprisings in Portuguese Guinea where 'liberation armies' are operating from Senegal and Guinea, as well as in Mozambique, not far removed from the Tanganyikan capital of Dar es Salaam which is regarded as the major centre for Communist subversion in southern Africa. Set about by mounting external pressure, Portugal might easily find herself with insufficient troops and resources to defend her colonial possessions. Then, perhaps, the Portuguese Government will come to the realization, like the other colonial powers before it, that rule of African territories from Europe is an anachronism.

XII

THE 'GRAND DOCTEUR'

LAMBARENÉ, SET ON the banks of the Ogowe River deep in the jungles of Equatorial Africa, is still today one of the more remote places on the African continent, although communications with the outside world have greatly improved since the year 1913 when Dr Albert Schweitzer first reached Lambarené by boat from Port Gentil on the coast of Gabon.

It was with a feeling of relief that we struck the Ogowe River some three or four miles upstream from the village of Lambarené. Throughout the three-hour flight from Brazzaville, capital of the ex-French Congo, we had had beneath us a limitless expanse of dense tropical rain-forest. If our engine had failed our best chance of survival would have been to ditch the aircraft in one of the numerous crocodile-infested streams that intersect the area. Not the most attractive prospect!

On landing at Lambarené's small airstrip we learned from the African in charge there that the only way of reaching Dr Schweitzer's hospital was to walk two miles to the river-bank, cross by the ferry to the island on which the village of Lambaréné stands, and find someone on the other side of the island to take us by *pirogue* (dug-out canoe) to the hospital about a mile upstream.

The setting sun, as it sank behind the jungle-covered hills of Lambaréné, momentarily turned the broad waters of the Ogowe River into a shimmering sheet of burnished gold. Then it was night. The elderly African propelled his flimsy craft with an increased vigour. He did not like paddling his canoe after dark for fear of shipwreck against the dark motionless mass of a hippopotamus. To avoid the swift current in mid-stream he hugged the bank under an overhang of branches and trailing creepers which reached almost to the water. On attaining the upstream end of the island he altered course and made for the opposite shore. Soon we were gliding in under the palm-trees that line the waterfront below the hospital and the canoe with a slight lurch came to rest on a sandy beach. Numerous small fires were flickering in the darkness; around each was huddled a group of Africans cooking their evening meal. By the light of the flames we were able to make out the long, low forms of the hospital-buildings of Lambaréné.

Before setting out for Africa I had gone to the Tropical Disease Hospital in north London to be inoculated against cholera, yellow fever, typhoid (A & B), typhus and tetanus. There I ran into Miss Olga Deterding who is a friend of Dr Schweitzer's and who has on several occasions gone out to Equatorial Africa to help as a nurse at the hospital. She told me that she was leaving for Lambaréné the next day and said that if our plane ever got as far as Gabon we should certainly look in on Dr Schweitzer.

As it was, it had taken Arnold and myself nearly three months to reach Lambaréné, and although I had sent her a cable from Brazzaville three days before, warning her of our arrival, I had no idea if she was still there. A figure clothed in white and surmounted by an enormous white sun-helmet emerged from a hospital-building; it was one of the European nurses. I asked her if Miss Deterding was still at the hospital, only to learn that she had left ten days before to return to Europe. Not wishing to impose ourselves on this great man just before dinner unannounced, we decided to make our way back to the village to see if we could find lodging for the night.

Just then Mlle Silver, a Dutch nurse who is among those who have been longest with Dr Schweitzer, appeared and greeted us warmly saying: 'We received your telegram and when we heard an aeroplane fly over after lunch we thought it was you; the Doctor insisted on going to meet you and set out in his *pirogue* to the airport where we waited for an hour or more. But it was not your plane that had arrived, so we came back to the hospital.' I was much embarrassed, supposing that Schweitzer had assumed from my cable that it was my grandfather arriving. Mlle Silver assured me that this had not been the case and led us by the light of a paraffin-lamp to a small but pleasant room furnished with two iron beds, a table, chair and wash-stand. She told us that dinner was at 7 p.m. but explained that 'hospital time', determined by the whim of the Doctor, was running half an hour behind local time. She said that we had best go by the bell that would be rung when dinner was ready. After bringing us a couple of paraffin-lamps she left us the key to our room, warning us to take particular care about locking the door because of the danger of theft. This parting admonition came as a surprise to the two of us. Only that morning we had been reproved for locking our hotel-room in Brazzaville. We had crossed the Congo River by ferry from Brazzaville to Leopoldville, where we had interviewed Mr Robert Gardiner, the able Ghanaian in charge of the United Nations operations in the Congo.

I had by mistake put the key to my hotel-room in my pocket and taken it with me. On returning to our hotel in Brazzaville, we found the French *patronne* in a tantrum. 'Why did you lock your room?' she demanded. 'These Africans aren't thieves!' Now here we were in Lambaréné being told to beware of thieves. One might expect robbery in the big city, but not in the village— particularly a village where a man as saintly as Schweitzer has devoted his life to the welfare of the local population. To find things otherwise is a disappointing reflection on human nature.

When the dinner-bell sounded we were shown to two empty places opposite Schweitzer who sat at the middle of a long wooden table. He jumped up from his place and shook us both firmly by the hand. The first thing he asked us was whether we had come by motor-boat or *pirogue*. When we replied the latter, a beaming smile of approval came over his face. It seems that this is one of the criteria by which the Doctor judges his guests. Dinner was attended by the thirty or more members of the hospital staff, all of whom were European with the exception of a Japanese doctor and his wife who run the nearby leper village. The two longer sides of the dining-hall were made of gauze netting designed to keep out the mosquitoes while at the same time allowing a breeze, should there be one, to pass through the room. But that evening there was not a breath of air. Lambaréné lies within fifty miles of the Equator, and the heat and humidity are oppressive. Sweat was running down the faces of those present, doctors and nurses alike.

As I was enjoying what I had assumed to be a piece of mutton, Schweitzer leant across the table and enquired: 'Eh! Bien, Monsieur Churchill, comment aimez-vous notre crocodile?' I smiled knowingly, confident that I was having my leg pulled. Thereupon the whole table, which seems rarely to join in the Doctor's dinner-conversation, roared with laughter at my disbelief.

Angola: remains of coffee farm after terrorist attack
OVERLEAF: *Lambaréné: waterfront*

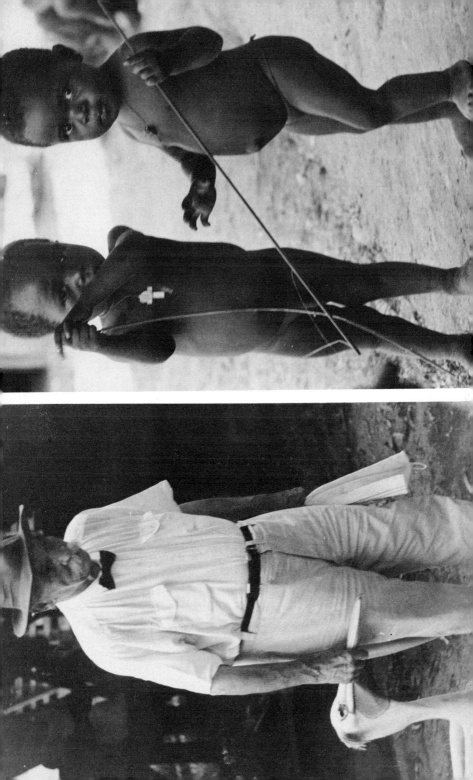

Schweitzer explained that crocodile was quite a delicacy in these parts, where fresh meat is rare. He told us that except for rice, which has to be imported, almost all the food for the hospital was grown locally, including bananas, mangoes, papayas and coffee, as well as that strange fruit—inevitably found on desert-islands by the treasure-hunting castaways of one's boyhood books —the bread-fruit, which in fact tastes more like potato. This is a much more practical idea than we had found prevailing at Brazzaville, our last port of call, where the head-waiter of a restaurant had excused the enormity of the bill by explaining that all the food had to be flown out three times a week by Air France from Paris.

After dinner the table was cleared and hymn-books were brought forward. The Doctor then announced a hymn in German and strode over to his old upright piano that stands at one side of the room. A dim paraffin-lamp lit his tousled grey hair, droopy moustache and ruddy complexion, as he played with a vigour truly remarkable in a man of eighty-eight. When the hymn was done the Doctor read a passage from the Bible and gave a brief and pointed explanation of the text he had read. Then all retired for the night.

In the early hours of the morning there was a violent thunder-storm, attended by a deluge of rain such as one only sees in the tropics. All was clearly lit up by the almost continuous flashes of lightning, and looking out through the gauze-covered side of our bedroom it was as if we were standing under the lip of a waterfall. However by the time the reveille-bell pealed out at 6.30 a.m. there was not a cloud in the sky and the sun was rising swiftly above the palm-trees.

Schweitzer's hospital stands on the side of a hill overlooking the broad Ogowe River. It is surrounded by the impenetrable primeval forest that encroaches on all sides. Here the visitor finds

Lambaréné: a view of the hospital
OVERLEAF: *Dr Schweitzer and pelican*
AND *Lambaréné: children from near-by village*

Africa as he has imagined it should be—a land of steaming, teeming rain-forest where massive trees and tumultuous jungle exclude the light of day and thwart the advance of civilization. The hospital at Lambarené is not out of character with its surroundings.

To those visitors who come to Lambarené expecting to find a clean and modern hospital, Dr Schweitzer's establishment is inevitably a surprise. Some 500 Africans are accommodated in the long, low hospital-buildings made of wood and corrugated iron. The buildings are divided by partitions into cubicles, each with its own entrance. The cubicles, in which the patients lie side by side on wooden bunks, present a dismal picture of darkness, dinginess and dirt. Outside on the doorstep sit those inmates who are less seriously ill, some of them deep in contemplation. Beside them are the dead embers of the fire on which they cooked their meal the previous evening; and on all sides there is a litter of wash-pots, cooking-pots, empty bottles and rusty tins. In the open drainage ditches that run beside the hospital-buildings slops, old bandages, banana skins and other refuse lie putrefying and stagnating in the sun. The hospital's only sanitary facilities are two latrines, kept under lock and key for the exclusive use of the European staff. They consist of two wooden huts standing side by side on an elevated platform supported by stilts over a ditch which is a seething mass of maggots and flies. The 500 or so Africans are supposed to do their business on the edge of the jungle, but most are sick and all are lazy, with the result that few get that far. There are certain things one associates with hospitals the world over, even those in the bush, namely: concrete floors, white-washed rooms, iron beds, electricity, lavatories, running water, covered drains, and that rather nasty smell of disinfectant —none of these are to be found in the African quarters of the hospital at Lambarené.

Dr Schweitzer explains that the African has a horror of European-type hospitals and he contends that it is only because he runs his hospital on the lines of a native village that so many Africans come to him for treatment. Many Africans, he says, would sooner suffer or even die, from lack of medical attention, rather than go to a European hospital with its unfamiliar, unfriendly, aseptic atmosphere. At Lambaréné they can have their families with them, they are allowed to go on wearing their own old clothes and they are able to live the life to which they are accustomed, while at the same time undergoing medical treatment. There is no doubt that this is why Africans come to Lambaréné rather than to the government-run hospital, situated not far away. And some come from 200 miles or more upstream by dug-out canoe or river-steamer to be treated at Schweitzer's hospital.

Soon after lunch on the day after our arrival we witnessed what seems to be a regular hospital ritual. A dozen or so bedraggled Africans, some of them armed with shovels, lined up before Schweitzer. He called them briskly to attention—an order not very briskly complied with—thereupon they removed their hats with a deep bow, and with grins on their faces they intoned: 'Bonjour, Grand Docteur!' Schweitzer, seeing us watching, blushed slightly and then chuckled in his merry way explaining that this was his labour force and he had to check that they were all present and correct. Most of the hospital patients bring with them at least one member of their family to act as their guardian and to cook for them. And the Doctor puts all the able-bodied men, including some of the lepers, to work at digging or some similar activity, which they perform with a singular lack of vigour. When the day's work is done they are given a ration of bananas or rice, and at the end of the week they receive a *cadeau* of a few pennies.

One afternoon, a Sunday, we took a *pirogue* and went with one of the German doctors at the hospital to the village of Abangue a couple of miles upstream. This small village, inhabited solely by Africans, was one of the most pleasant that we saw in all of Africa. A broad grass path lined on either side by clean, well-constructed huts led up from the landing-place where brightly-coloured butterflies flitted by the water's edge. The first hut had a great fishing-net hung up outside to dry in the sun. The owner invited us in and proudly showed us the masks—most sinister in appearance—that he was making for the Saturday night dances that take place in the village. Next door was a man who repaired clocks and radios. And further along a man with a sewing-machine was sitting outside his house mending some clothes. The huts, which were built of palm-trees, had big windows and were furnished with locally-made tables and chairs. In one of the huts there were two pretty girls reading through a pile of note-books. They told us that they were both married to the local school-teacher and were correcting some French home-work done by the children. The father of one of the girls was sitting outside the house relaxing in the sun. We sat down on the ground beside him and had a long talk which ranged from local politics to how much one has to pay for a wife. He had some very sound ideas. After telling us that the average price for a wife was £15, he went on to say: 'It's all right for you Europeans to lead a bachelor existence, you have servants to look after you and cook for you. We do not. Instead we have to buy a wife. But it's no use having just one wife. You need at least two, so that if one gets sick there is still one to look after you.'

For several years now, members of the hospital staff have been urging Schweitzer to build a new air-conditioned operating-theatre. They say that the present one with its gauze sides lets the dust in from outside and gets so hot that two nurses are required to mop the surgeon's brow to prevent the sweat falling on to the patient on the operating-table. The Doctor was eventually persuaded that this would be a good idea and the concrete foundations for the new building were laid. However it seems that Schweitzer, perhaps because of his dislike for modern machines and equipment, had delayed the project in favour of an extension to the guest-accommodation. But, as one of the staff told me: 'Everything is relative. There is no point having a modern, air-conditioned operating-theatre if the patient, as soon as he returns to his cubicle, is going to pull the dressing aside and poke around with his finger to see what has been done to him. Although we use the latest drugs and the most modern surgical techniques it is really eighteenth century medicine that we are practising here.'

The doctors and nurses at Lambarené are mostly Dutch, Swiss or German, and many are very highly qualified. However, except for a couple of the nurses who have been with the Doctor for a long time, most of the staff come for a period of two or three years; and there seems to be no trusted lieutenant or chosen successor who could carry on the hospital when the Doctor is gone. Working at the hospital at the time of our visit were a young American couple in their mid-twenties; he was a doctor from North Carolina, she a nurse. After reading of Dr Schweitzer's greatness and hearing of his renown, they had decided to devote their lives, or at least a major part of them, to the service of the great Doctor in Lambarené. They had thereupon sold everything they had in America and taken a boat for Africa. Now, within a year of their arrival, they were planning to leave Lambarené. They felt that all initiative towards improving the conditions at the hospital was being stifled and they seemed sadly disillusioned. This couple were doubtless an exception. The majority of the staff seem to enjoy their time at Lambarené, not only for the vast amount of practical experience they accumulate, but because working among people so in need of their skills must be most rewarding.

Dr Schweitzer's reputation is so great that at the snap of his fingers untold resources from the great American charitable foundations, no less than from his many admirers throughout the world, could be available for the modernization of his hospital. Yet it is his wish to keep Lambaréné as he originally conceived it. He has built the hospital and the nearby leper-village largely with his own hands from such materials as could be obtained locally. He was thirty-eight years old when he first came to Lambaréné and already he was a doctor four times over, in theology, philosophy, music and medicine. He had written two authoritative works, one on Bach, the other on organ-building, besides a handful of other books on Christ and civilization; and an academic career full of promise seemed to lie before him. Yet he turned his back on it as he says in his autobiography: 'in order to devote myself from that time forward to the direct service of humanity'. He is very conscious of this 'act of renunciation' and later in his book asserts: 'There are no heroes of action: only heroes of renunciation and suffering. But few of them are known, and even these not to the crowd, but to the few.' Perhaps the most obvious exception to this rule is Schweitzer himself.

When he first came to Lambaréné there was no other doctor for hundreds of miles around and an epidemic of sleeping-sickness was at its height. For want of medical attention the local people were dying on all sides from this and other diseases. It was no mean achievement to found a hospital of any kind in the heart of the jungles of Equatorial Africa. That was in 1913.

Half a century has passed since then. Africa has changed immeasurably in those fifty years: Schweitzer and Lambaréné have altered but little. He has weathered well. During all his time in tropical Africa he has never contracted any serious disease. And today, in his ninetieth year, the 'Grand Docteur' is still a tower of strength. Sun-helmet on, he stands for hours beneath the equatorial sun directing some new building project or resolving a dispute in the hospital. And in the evening, when darkness has fallen on Lambarené and the sounds of the jungle are silent, the glow of a paraffin-lamp shines out from the tiny room where, amid a rummage of papers, books and tools, he sits at his table writing late into the night, in the cause of civilization and peace. Lambarené remains a corner of Africa unspoiled as yet by the advance of the modern world—a back-water cut off from the mainstream of the African Revolution.

XIII

THE WHITE MAN'S GRAVE

ONE DAY'S FLYING brought us from the heart of the rain-forests of Equatorial Africa to the southern fringe of the Sahara. On the way we made a brief stop at the exotic mountainous island of Fernando Po where we ate the lunch we had been given before leaving Lambaréné, consisting of mango-jam sandwiches and giant bananas which had been packed in a small white linen bag marked in indelible ink with the initials 'A.S.' Then we set a northerly course up across the Cameroons towards Fort Lamy, capital of the Tchad. After our leaving behind the Gulf of Guinea and Mount Cameroon, surmounted by cumulus clouds towering to 40,000 ft or more, the dense jungle beneath us began to give way to the more arid open grasslands of the Sudan that stretch the width of the continent from the Ethiopian foothills to the west coast.

Fort Lamy, together with Kano, Gao and Timbuktu, is one of

Lambaréné: leper village

the southern termini of the trans-Sahara caravan routes. Only a few miles to the north the last stunted blade of grass is passed and the desert proper begins. From that point, until the Mediterranean coast is reached, there is nothing but a vast expanse of sand and rocky waste. The desert holds a peculiar fascination for those who have come to know it, and exercises within them a yearning to return to its silence and solitude. Making one's way across a seemingly limitless sea of sand under the relentless glare of the noon-day sun, or lying awake beneath the clustered myriads of stars and seeing, in the cold crystalline clarity of the night-air, the whole universe revolving overhead, the hopes and fears of the world seem remote, yet the Infinite lies within one's grasp.

In the course of the expedition I had made to the Tibesti Mountains in 1961 I had made the acquaintance of Colonel Baylon, a French Army officer serving in the Tchad. Heading northwards from the desert trading-centre of Faya, the southern-most point reached by the expedition, we had got lost in a *ghibli* (sandstorm). Only after three days did we get back on to the track which was erratically signposted with empty oil-drums and parched camel-carcasses; by then we had used up half our water-supply and were strictly rationed to six pints per day. Six pints of water is not as much as it sounds when the temperature is over 110°F in the shade and one is continuously digging out vehicles that have sunk up to their axles in soft sand. When the sun broke the eastern horizon on our fourth day out of Faya, the expedition's five Land Rovers had been advancing in line-abreast across the open desert for the previous two hours, after making an early start so as to reach the next water-hole before our water ran out. As the first rays of the sun were thawing out our bodies, chilled by the pre-dawn air which was little above the freezing-point, we sighted three puffs of dust on the horizon ahead. The dust-clouds grew rapidly in size and through binoculars we could see three large Power Wagons with a machine-gun mounted on each advancing towards us. It was an army patrol consisting of a score of Tchad soldiers whose faces were hidden behind large dark goggles and scarves which were wrapped around their mouths and noses as a protection against the sand. Colonel Baylon, the officer in charge of the patrol, dismounted and came over to greet us. We set up a collapsible table and some chairs in the middle of the desert and sat down to breakfast. The Colonel produced a bottle of Dubonnet and some cigars, while we managed to find some whisky. After a rather lively meal the Colonel's patrol headed south in a swirl of dust and we went on our way, leaving a few empty bottles in the desert to supplement the inadequate signposts along the route.

When therefore Arnold and I landed at Fort Lamy the first thing I did was to telephone French Army Headquarters to enquire if Colonel Baylon was still in the country. By good fortune he was in Fort Lamy itself and I got through to him right away. He told us not to move from the airport, he would be there. Five minutes later a camouflaged staff car drew up outside the airport building and the Colonel, who we found out had been promoted to become commanding officer of all the forces in the Tchad, drove us back to his house in the suburbs of Fort Lamy on the banks of the Chari River. Although it was already late in the afternoon he insisted on laying on lunch for the two of us and with a deep military bark to his batman ordered: 'Allez vite! Apportez whisky: champagne: foie gras!' Seeing the relish with which we put away all this and more besides, he looked on approvingly and punctuated the arrival of each course with interjections of 'C'est bon!' (pronounced 'bong', Marseilles-style). He told us that he was leaving at dawn the following morning by air for Bardai, one of the oases in the Tibesti Mountains that I had visited two years before, and he invited us to come along with him. I was sorely tempted to accept his offer but in the end we decided to continue on our way west to Nigeria. After lunch we visited Camp Koufra, the army barracks from which General Leclerc and the Free French had begun their march up across the Sahara to join the Allied Armies in the western desert during World War II.

Early the next morning we drove to the airport with Colonel Baylon who had kindly put both of us up for the night. We thanked the Colonel for his hospitality and took off for Kano, the ancient walled city of Northern Nigeria. Kano's Moslem influence is pronounced. The long loose galabia of the Arab-world is much in evidence and the mosque, with its green dome and minarets, occupies a central position in the city. In Nigeria's northern region, Moslem Emirs wield extensive political power locally and some, like the Sardauna of Sokoto who leads the Northern Peoples' Congress Party, exercise a decisive influence on Nigeria's national politics. The Sardauna, in a radio interview broadcast in Britain recently, even went so far as to refer to the Federal Prime Minister, Sir Abubakar Tafawa Balewa, as 'my Prime Minister'.

It was nearly dusk when we touched down at Lagos, the Nigerian capital. We asked the only taxi-driver waiting at the airport how much he would charge to drive us to a hotel in the centre of town. With a disbelieving grin on his face he replied: 'Five pounds!' I countered with: 'One pound ten.' In the end we settled for £2 and the driver seemed delighted. We soon discovered that the Lagos taxi-drivers have a strong aversion to the meters installed in their vehicles and need much coaxing to be persuaded to use them. No less than three taxi-drivers during our brief stay in Lagos insisted that their meters were broken; another, with more candour, told us he did not like his because it did not charge enough money.

To the traveller who has been to the Rhodesias and South Africa it is surprising and refreshing to see how the British in Nigeria, Ghana, Sierra Leone and the Gambia mix freely with the Africans. The reason for this remarkably different attitude is not far to seek; it stems from a radically different historical background. The high plateau that stretches up through South, Central and East Africa, at about 5,000 ft above sea-level, enjoys a temperate climate and consists mostly of open grasslands and bush: as a result the European came to this area as a settler. West Africa, on the other hand, is mostly low-lying and the hot humid climate of the Guinea Coast made it a breeding-ground for mosquitoes carrying malaria and other tropical diseases. Here, except for a handful of missionaries, the European came to trade, not to settle. Europeans have been trading with West Africa for the last 500 years; the commodities they came in search of are reflected in the names they gave to various parts of the coastline, namely the Slave Coast (Nigeria), the Gold Coast (Ghana) and the Ivory Coast, which still bears the name given to it by the early traders. It is only since the end of the last century with the aid of modern technology and medicine that Africa's more lethal diseases have been eliminated or at least checked; until that time the area fully lived up to its name—the White Man's Grave.

It is an important fact that the West African came to know the European first of all as a business-man and latterly as an administrator—never as a colonist. Unlike eastern and southern Africa where the European settlers had a large say in the running of their countries, West Africa was governed almost entirely by officials sent out from Europe on short-term appointments. There were none of the problems posed by the European ownership of land, nor were there any 'settlers' interests' to be taken into account. And in the British West African colonies at least, it was always accepted that the eventual aim was to train the Africans for self-government. This has made for a much easier relationship between black and white in West Africa than was possible elsewhere on the continent.

On the day after our arrival in Lagos we lunched with the British High Commissioner Lord Head, who has since been posted to Singapore as High Commissioner to the Malaysian Federation. At lunch, which was outside beside a swimming-pool, I found myself sitting next to a very pretty Nigerian girl who told me that she had just returned from England where she had done a course in nursing. She was now teaching other trainee nurses in a Lagos hospital. Arnold and I almost regretted being in such good health. In the afternoon we went to see Lagos' large and very squalid market where we found monkey skulls and hands for sale together with other equally desirable objects used as ju-jus or charms. We then made a visit to a museum where we saw stone and bronze work, much of which comes from the ancient city of Benin. Many of the objects from Benin are believed to pre-date European arrival on the West African coast and for this reason they are of great interest.

That evening Arnold and I went to one or two of Lagos' open-air night-clubs. The dance-floors were packed with blacks and whites swaying to and fro. In time to a reverberating rhythm on the drums, the dancers jogged around in a circle to the step of the 'High Life', the local West African dance. Here African and European seemed completely at ease with one another and the atmosphere was the gayest and most relaxed that we found anywhere on the continent.

Nigeria, with a population of 56 million, is by far the largest nation in Africa and on gaining her independence in October 1960 she became the third most populous member of the Commonwealth. A country like Ghana, with less than one seventh the population of Nigeria, might kick up a big song and dance. But high-pitched, high-flown sentiments with a hollow ring do little to impress the young nations of Africa; they are looking for concrete achievements which they can emulate. Nigeria, both by her size and by her example of getting on with the job without unnecessary hot air, has become the pace-setter in Africa. For this reason the success or failure of Nigeria's experiment in democracy has great import for the future of Western ideals on the African continent.

Modern democracy is a highly complex form of government that it has taken Englishmen, by trial and error, nearly a thousand years to evolve. And even among those who believe firmly in democracy, there is considerable doubt that it is suited to the needs of Africa in its present stage of development. It is contended that in a society where the great majority of the population is uneducated, ignorant and poor, democracy is unable to provide the necessary stability and that a more forceful and authoritarian form of government is required to get a developing country's economy off the ground. But there are others, particularly in Nigeria, who grasp the larger hope and believe that Africa can avoid the misery of arbitrary and tyrannical governments and take a short-cut to democracy. They cite the continued tribal basis of African society as a bulwark against dictatorship. For it is still broadly true to say that in the greater part of the continent, despite the efforts of nationalist leaders, the African votes not so much for the representative of a political party, as for a representative of his tribe. A federal system of government such as Nigeria's which respects the tribal basis of a country is less likely to produce a dictator than is a unitary system such as in Ghana where tribalism is discouraged.

Nigeria is composed of four main tribes and divided into four regions: the Hausa and Fulani in the Northern Region, the Yoruba in the West and Mid-West, and the Ibo in the East. The present government is formed by a coalition of the ruling parties of the Eastern and Northern Regions. The federation was presented with its first major crisis in November 1962 when Chief Awolowo, leader of the opposition Action Group, was charged in the High Court at Lagos with treasonable felony, having previously been removed from his position as Prime Minister of the Western Region. In September 1963 Awolowo and his deputy, Chief Enahoro, were sentenced to ten and fifteen years in jail respectively.

The idea of a 'loyal opposition' is utterly baffling to the vast majority of Africans; they regard it as a totally self-contradictory proposition. We were able to get some idea of the difficulties involved when we were told in Accra that in all the twenty-six native languages in use in Ghana today, the only word to translate 'opposition' is 'enemy' and the 'leader of the opposition' therefore becomes the 'chief enemy'. To a party elected to power on a popular vote, any opposition appears to be a defiance of the declared wishes of the people and is therefore judged treasonable. While to a party that is unsuccessful at the elections it seems evident that there is something wrong with the whole system and it is soon decided to have resort to the old *assagai* and *panga*, or more modern weapons if they are available (which they all too often are). And in the end, whether it is a question of the opposition plotting the overthrow of the government, or of the government looking for an excuse to lock up the opposition, becomes impossible to say. It all boils down to the old question: 'Which was first—the chicken or the egg?'

Despite the many obstacles that confront a democracy in Africa, Nigeria seems to have weathered her first constitutional storm in relatively good order. But these are early days yet: troubled waters lie ahead. Africa is passing through the storms of revolution and being thrown about by a swelling sea of discontent. For many years to come, until her economic problems are solved, Africa's political barometer will be set at 'changeable'.

Nigeria is engaged in an all-out drive to raise the standard of living of her people by the development of the country's natural and human resources. The Minister for Commerce and Industry, Mr Dipcharima, told us of Nigeria's ambitious six-year plan which involves the expenditure of £676 million by 1968. One of the major items of capital development will be the Kainji Dam and hydro-electric scheme in the northern part of the country which, for an estimated cost of £68 million, will generate three times as much power as Kariba. Other projects include extensions to Nigeria's road and rail networks, an iron and steel mill, an oil refinery and the development of agriculture and mineral resources. Dipcharima, a large and jovial Nigerian, said that a substantial part of the capital was being provided by Nigeria herself; the rest by the World Bank, foreign governments and 'my friends in the City'.

In the field of education too, Nigeria is setting her sights high. In 1962 there were more than 3 million children attending her schools; and by 1970 it is planned to have some 8,000 secondary-school teachers, half of them Nigerian. Mr Jack Thornton, an expatriate British civil servant attached to the External Aid Bureau of the Nigerian Ministry of Education, had high praise for the 300 Peace Corps teachers at work in the country. (This figure has risen to over 500 at the time of writing.) But he regretted the fact that to a Commonwealth country of 56 million people Britain's Voluntary Service Overseas (V.S.O.) had only been able to send eighteen graduate and thirty-six non-graduate volunteers. V.S.O. began in 1958 as a voluntary movement with a limited amount of Government financial backing and it provided to some extent the model for the United States Peace Corps set up by President Kennedy three years later. But by 1963 there were only 255 V.S.O. volunteers, less than half of them graduates, on the job abroad compared to over 5,000 of the Peace Corps. Little is known in Britain of V.S.O.—during three years at a British university I had never once heard of the organization. Lack of funds has hampered a large-scale expansion of its activities but most important of all as Mr Thornton told me: 'V.S.O. must be given status.'

A tentative move in this direction was made in February 1964 when it was announced that the Duke of Edinburgh had agreed to become President of a Council for Volunteers Overseas. At the same time the Government announced its intention of increasing its contribution from £270,000 in 1964 to £650,000 in 1965—a miserable pittance amounting to less than a fiftieth of the Peace Corps' £35 million budget. The number of volunteers is to be raised to 1,300 by 1965, when it is expected that the Peace Corps will be 14,000 strong. In the developing countries there is a crying need for man-to-man assistance on these lines. One individual who goes to help raise a country's standard of education, to improve methods of agriculture or to impart technical know-how, is of incomparably greater value to a backward people than many thousands of dollars in financial aid which all too often finds its way into the pockets of corrupt officials.

Man-to-man aid is both the cheapest and the most effective way of helping a country. And this is a field in which Britain can, and as the head of the Commonwealth has a duty to, play a full and active role. The financial resources could easily be made available and the human resources are waiting to be tapped. That there is a vast well of idealism among Britain's youngsters is shown by the large numbers prepared to sit on their tails in Trafalgar Square waving Ban-the-Bomb placards. It is time that their doubtless well-intentioned energies be directed towards a more useful and productive cause. But there is no reason that the

project be confined to Britain alone. What about a Commonwealth Corps? Nothing could do more to strengthen the tenuous
links of the British Commonwealth than that its youngsters
should unite to eradicate the mass misery that afflicts the greater
part of the Commonwealth's 750 million people. The Commonwealth is not a matriarchy tied to Britain's apron-strings: it is
a brotherhood of free sovereign nations. The countries of the
Commonwealth have stood loyally by Britain and the soldiers of
all of them have fought at her side in two world wars. Now it is
for Britain to give her less fortunate brethren a hand in their
war—the war against poverty, disease and ignorance. The more
prosperous countries such as Britain, Canada, Australia and New
Zealand could join together to form and finance a formidable
army of volunteers. And the less developed nations could themselves contribute volunteers to work in their own countries side
by side with the main body of the Commonwealth Corps. Such
co-operation would give the Commonwealth a new sense of
mission and a new meaning in the world.

*   *   *

Much of the flight westwards along the coast from Lagos to
Lomé, the capital of Togo, was made at an average altitude of
ten feet above sea-level. Just off our right wing-tip an endless
golden beach which shelved up steeply towards a thick tangle
of palm-trees flashed by as we skimmed along the coastline at
180 m.p.h. a matter of inches above the crests of the great rollers
that were pounding the shore. Here and there a dark cluster of
dug-out canoes lying on the beach ahead would announce a small
fishing village consisting of a few huts set up against the palm-
trees. As we flew by, the fishermen sitting on the sand repairing
their casting-nets would look up in surprise and wave, while the

children in a state of wild excitement rushed down the beach towards us. Once or twice the menacing crest of a mammoth wave reared up above our left wing-tip forcing us to pull back sharply on the control-column to avoid being swamped. Climbing a little we banked to the right and then turned back on to course to fly parallel to the coast about a mile inland. Here we were over mangrove swamps and calm lagoons which had what looked like wicker barriers erected across them to trap fish. At one point we flew over a dug-out canoe to photograph some fishermen casting in the shallow waters of a lagoon. They waved to us as we approached but, to our surprise, when we looked back the canoe was empty. Then a second or two later some heads bobbed to the surface and it was evident that the crew had abandoned ship. Thereafter we climbed to a more respectable altitude and soon after, touched down at Lomé. In Nigeria we had been told that because of the assassination only a month before (13 January 1963) of the Togolese President, Sylvanus Olympio, we would have difficulty getting into the country without a visa. As it happened, we were not even asked to show our passports. And it is a remarkable fact that in the whole of our journey, which took us to more than forty countries, neither Arnold nor myself ever once had our baggage opened by the Customs at an airport.

The chief object of our visit to Togo was to find out how President Olympio, one of Africa's most outstanding political leaders, had come to be murdered. Besides being a highly educated man speaking English, French and German, Olympio had been a shrewd economist. Togo, a former German colony, had been administered by France until 1960 when it became independent. Not long after independence Olympio decided to break his ties with the French Community, a loose association of France's former West African colonies established by General de Gaulle in 1958. The French Community is a device by which

France obtains defence agreements, often involving the presence of French troops as in the Tchad, a lion's share of the former colony's export and import trade and fourteen votes at the U.N. to boot. In return France provides these nations with generous technical assistance and a budget subsidy that averages about £5 per head of population each year. Having forgone this budget subsidy from France to obtain Togo's complete independence, Olympio was forced to introduce an austerity programme. This involved increasing the working week from forty to forty-five hours without any rise in wages and reducing the price the farmer obtained for his coffee from 65 Frs to 60 Frs per kilo, the difference going into a development fund.

At the same time he refused to increase the Togolese Army to more than one company. Togo's soldiers were drawn mostly from the Cabré, a warlike tribe of the north, from which France had recruited a considerable number of troops for service in Algeria. When these soldiers returned to Togo in the summer of 1962 they found themselves out of a job. Discontented, they made representations to the President. It seems that Olympio sought, and obtained, from the United States Government a promise to finance a second army company. However it is believed that the American Ambassador subsequently talked him out of the idea. When therefore the soldiers returned, having drawn up a list of their grievances on paper, Olympio tore the document up in their faces. It was then that they planned the *coup* which appears to have been aimed at coercing the President rather than overthrowing him. The next evening the soldiers drove up to Olympio's residence, sprayed the building with bullets, but found it deserted. Apparently he had fled to the adjoining U.S. Embassy compound and hidden himself in a car for the night. The whole area was surrounded by about fifty mutinous soldiers. The next morning the American Ambassador got up at six a.m. to check that all was in order in the compound. In so doing he must have passed close to the car where Olympio was hiding; some suggest he may even have talked with him. Mme Olympio was then sent by the mutineers to tell her husband that if he gave himself up his safety would be assured. After a brief conversation with Olympio she returned through the Embassy to inform the soldiers that he was prepared to surrender. However the soldiers meanwhile came round another way. It is thought they had been drinking to keep their courage up and when they found Olympio they dragged him out of the car and shot him.

Like the more recent army mutinies in Tanganyika, Uganda and Kenya in January 1964, there is no reason to suspect any sinister political motives. The Togolese mutineers certainly had no plans for taking over the government of the country and when they sobered up they appeared almost to regret what they had done. As it was, several days passed before anyone thought of forming a government. In the end the suggestion that this might be a good idea seems to have come from the neighbouring state of Dahomey. The man who headed the new government was Olympio's brother-in-law, a Togolese called Nicholas Grunitzky who is half Polish by birth. When I went to interview him in the presidential office he told me that his prime concern was to maintain order. 'We don't want,' he said, 'to give other countries (by which he evidently meant Ghana) or the *casques bleus* (United Nations) a chance to intervene here.'

*   *   *

Ghana, with an average *per capita* income approaching £100 a year (compared to about £30 in Nigeria and £14 in Somalia) is one of the most prosperous states in Africa. Her wealth is based primarily on the fact that she grows one third of the world's production of cocoa which accounts for 70 per cent of her exports. Besides this she produces manganese and diamonds as well as gold from the old Ashanti mines. When the Volta River Dam project financed largely by the United States is completed, much of the power will be used to produce aluminium from local bauxite. The wealth of the country enabled the British colonial administration to spend more money here than in other colonies on educating the people, who already had a good grounding as a result of 500 years of contact with Europe and the efforts of the missionaries on the coast. Because of this the Ghanaians are today among the best educated and most prosperous of Africans. They are an able, intelligent and likeable people. But their present government is an affront both to their intelligence and to their dignity.

Ghana provides a classic example of the one-man-one-vote-once type of democracy that threatens to spread to other African countries. Dr (short for Dictator) Kwame Nkrumah is known to his lackeys and the hack Ghana press by the title of *Osagyefo* (Saviour). What he is attempting to save is not exactly clear—some suggest it is his own skin. Be that as it may, in the seven years he has been in power he has effectively stripped the Ghanaian people of their constitutional rights and even of such civil liberties as they had enjoyed under British rule. On 4 November 1963 a Preventive Detention (Amendment) Bill became law, empowering the President to extend the period of a detention order at any time before its expiry for a further five-year period. This means that a citizen can be kept in jail without a trial indefinitely. On 11 December 1963 President Nkrumah dismissed Ghana's Chief Justice Sir Arku Korsah for failing to convict three of the defendants in a treason trial case. A spurious seal of legality was set on this act six weeks later with a referendum that gave the President the right to dismiss any High Court judge and made Nkrumah's Convention Peoples Party the only legal political body in the country. The result—a 99·9 per cent victory for Nkrumah—came as a surprise to no one. Many of the 'No' ballot-boxes had been sealed and extensive intimidation had been resorted to. On the first day of voting for instance, the party's morning newspaper gave a front-page warning: 'Those who think they can hide under the so-called "secrecy" of the polling booth to fool us must know that the days when we could be fooled are gone.'

An interesting footnote to these proceedings appeared in the *Ghana News Bulletin*, published by the Ghanaian High Commission in London; it followed its announcement of the dismissal of the Chief Justice by a report of a statement on the fifteenth anniversary of the Universal Declaration of Human Rights. The speaker, according to the report:

> reaffirmed Ghana's belief in human dignity and renewed the country's resolution to work for the establishment of peace and friendship among nations. . . . Genuine peace must be animated by justice and tolerance. . . . As you celebrate this day, we should look forward to a brighter and better future for mankind, when the principles underlying the Declaration of Human Rights will become the guiding spirit of the fundamental laws of all nations.

The speaker was none other than President Nkrumah.

Nkrumah's repressive legislation certainly does not give the impression of a popular leader ruling by the willing consent of a large majority. Perhaps with some reason, he has become afraid of his own people. He rarely ventures out of Flagstaff House, his official (and heavily guarded) residence in Accra. When he does, it is with a strong police escort that keeps the crowds well back. He has put away many of Ghana's most able citizens on trumped-

Ivory Coast: 'child sacrifice'

up charges. His frequent vituperations against the 'colonialists, neo-colonialists and economic imperialists' have done little to encourage the foreign investment that is so badly needed for the development of Ghana's resources, and he has saddled the country's economy with numerous costly and uneconomic projects. One of these was the purchase of a fleet of Russian Ilyushin turbo-prop airliners, similar to the Viscount. As we drove up to Accra Airport there were three of these aircraft standing idle on the tarmac. When I asked our Ghanaian taxi-driver what he thought of them he replied with some bitterness: 'They're not Ilyushins—they're Illusions.'

From Accra we flew to Kumasi, the old Ashanti capital, to visit Mr Joe Appiah, a distinguished Ghanaian lawyer who is married to the daughter of the British politician Sir Stafford Cripps. Appiah had done his best in 1956 to persuade the British Colonial Secretary Sir Alan Lennox-Boyd of the dangers of establishing a unitary, as opposed to a federal, constitution in Ghana, fearing that it would pave the way to a dictatorship. Having failed to achieve this, he became prominent in opposition to Nkrumah and, for his trouble, was thrown into jail. His release had come only two months before we went to see him at his house which stands in a small garden near the centre of Kumasi. He greeted us wearing an Ashanti toga-type garment. He had a sombre expression on his face and he apologized for the fact that he would have to leave after lunch to attend the funeral of a friend of his. The friend, a Cambridge graduate aged thirty-eight, had died in prison. The cause of his death was not disclosed: Nkrumah's police had merely contacted the dead man's family and had told them to come and collect the body.

'Kwame Nkrumah is to Africa today what Lenin was to the Soviet Union in 1917', Ghana's Minister of Defence announced with pride recently. Nevertheless Nkrumah's march towards

Ivory Coast: 'débutantes' prepared for circumcision

totalitarian socialism has so far done little to subdue the high spirits of the Ghanaian people. In Accra the lights are bright, the beat is loud and lively, the girls are pretty and the mood is festive. It is clear that Ghana prefers the High Life.

XIV

HOME ACROSS THE SAHARA

Aɪx-ᴇɴ-Pʀᴏᴠᴇɴᴄᴇ brought to Africa is perhaps the simplest way of describing Abidjan, capital of the ex-French colony of Ivory Coast. It is a remarkable fact there are today more French in Abidjan alone, than there are British in all of Ghana. This soon becomes apparent to someone arriving from the Commonwealth countries of West Africa; and it comes as a surprise to find that the shop-assistants and hotel-receptionists are not African, but European. There is none of the hustle and bustle of Lagos or Accra; there is none of the squalor of other African capitals— there is also none of the gaiety and colour. Tall concrete buildings, tree-lined avenues, street-side cafés, public gardens and playing fountains make Abidjan seem more like a provincial town of southern France than anything in Africa. The fact is that Abidjan, as its inhabitants readily admit and even proudly proclaim, is a *Ville Européene*: the *Ville Indigène*, where most of the city's

African population lives, is a separate and much less attractive affair. Because of its greater size or perhaps because of a fundamental difference in attitude, the French community in Abidjan keeps much more to itself than do the British inhabitants of West Africa. The *patron* of our hotel was taken aback when we asked him where there was an African night-club. He told us that there was no such thing and suggested instead that we try the 'Hi-Fi' which we found to be a subterranean, pseudo-Parisian *discothèque* stinking of air-conditioned sweat. Here, among the press of Europeans, we came across a handful of *evolués*—Africans who have been to France and who have returned Frenchmen in all but name; they are completely accepted by the European community and indeed feel more at home in the *Ville Européene* than in the *Ville Indigène*.

It is indicative of the relative impact of British and French culture that in Lagos and Accra the European dances the African 'High Life', while in Abidjan the African dances the 'Cha-cha-cha' and the 'Twist'. The British, as a race, have little culture and such as they have is unexportable. French culture on the other hand has exerted a profound influence on the manners, taste and outlook of the peoples with which it has come into contact—from North America to the Far East and from the Middle East to Africa. The *evolué*, whether he is from the Lebanon or the Ivory Coast, shares a common taste for expensive clothes and excellent cooking. And it is usually a safe bet that a French-speaking African cooks like a Frenchman. Needless to say that the English-speaking African cooks like the English; this might have been something best left at home.

It is in West Africa that the various stages of the African Revolution can most clearly be seen. In the jungle belt that stretches from the heart of the continent through West Africa there still exist many primitive and superstitious tribes who have had little contact with the outside world and whose life is little different from what it was centuries ago. But outside this belt the dress, language and religion of the African population reflect the profound influence of alien cultures: that of the Arab in the grasslands of the Sudan and that of the European in the coastal regions. Many of the Africans on the coast have turned their backs on tribal life. Some of them have become completely Europeanized and it is they who form the new ruling *élite*. There is however a far greater number that have been less fortunate and, having abandoned their traditional African existence, have found themselves unable to afford the European way of life to which they would aspire. They have therefore become part of a large body of unemployed and discontented city-dwellers that presents a grave threat to the stability of most African governments. This is a situation that seems bound to get worse before it gets better. And until the number of jobs available can in some measure keep pace with the number of school-leavers, the present large-scale expansion in education can only aggravate the problem. This is fertile ground for the seeds of subversion and it cannot be doubted that both the Soviet Union and China will do their best to exploit it. Comrade Chou-En-lai was confident, and doubtless correct, in his prediction during his visit to Somalia that '1964 will be a good year for Revolution'. Such a statement can scarcely have done much to reassure his African hosts as to the object of his safari on their continent.

The contrast between the modern European city of the coast and the primitive jungle of the interior is enormous; and it was the great advantage of having our own aircraft that we were able to escape from the big cities and visit some of the more remote parts of Africa. Three hundred miles north-west of Abidjan near the small administrative centre of Man deep in the jungles of Ivory Coast, we saw some of the most remarkable tribal dancing to be found anywhere on the continent. The dancing took place in a small village of palm-thatched mud-huts that stood in a jungle clearing. Throbbing drum-beats called the villagers together and they formed themselves into a circle about thirty feet in diameter. Three young girls, six or seven years old, with their bodies daubed with white paint and covered with beads, were led into the circle by two men carrying long pointed daggers. One of the men wiped the blade of his dagger with a leopard-skin that was tied to his waist, while the other rubbed his with what looked like a piece of monkey's tail. (It is common practice for parts of animals to be used as ju-jus or charms, although more powerful forms of Black Magic usually call for the use of human bodies.) As the drums beat faster the man with the leopard-skin seized one of the little girls and tossed her high into the air. The child's body, rigid and horizontal, for a moment seemed suspended on air. Then, as the body began to fall, the second man raised his dagger above his head so that the child's stomach fell on the point of the naked blade.

We had heard that child-sacrifice had been a frequent ritual among many African tribes in the old days, but this seemed horribly like the real thing. However Arnold and I were soon assured that the practice had been abandoned by this particular tribe all of thirty years ago and that what we were seeing was merely a demonstration of how it used to be done. Taking a closer look, we could see that as soon as the child's stomach fell on the point of the blade the man pulled the dagger downwards as fast as the child was falling; at the last minute he slipped the blade underneath and caught the child in his arms. It was certainly an act requiring great precision and skill, but it was reassuring to know that it was only an act.

Rather more sinister was the case of some of our fellow spectators. Standing in the crowd beside us were a dozen young girls who looked about seventeen years old but who were probably several years younger. They were naked from the waist up and the upper parts of their bodies were covered with white paste. The elder women of the tribe had made up the girls' faces using charcoal and red earth to make macabre designs on the white paste. These were the local 'débutantes', all set for their 'coming out party'—African style. But there were no girlish giggles to be heard and their faces under their heavy make-up were, in an eerie way, expressionless. We soon learned the reason —they were about to undergo the tribal ritual of circumcision.

Even in the rapidly changing Africa of today tribal customs, which to a Westerner might seem uncivilized or even a trifle barbaric, have been slow to die. And Mr Kenyatta, for instance, in his book entitled *Facing Mount Kenya* has staunchly defended the practice of female circumcision among his own Kikuyu tribe. In Basutoland there have been several cases in recent years of 'medicine murder' in which certain parts have been cut from the bodies of the innocent victims while they are still alive in order to make a powerful 'medicine' for use in Black Magic. Cannibalism seems to be on the decline although as recently as 1950 an African lawyer representing the Ivory Coast in the French Senate disappeared in the jungle—a court enquiring into the matter, after examining his mortal remains, came to the conclusion that he had been eaten by cannibals. In many parts of Africa European civilization is little more than a veneer. Beneath the surface there lies a twilight jungle of superstition where the sinister drum-beat of the Dark Continent can still be heard; it re-echoes among the descendants of the slaves across the ocean, as *voodoo* in the islands of the West Indies and as *macumba* deep in the forests of Brazil.

It had been our intention to fly north to Bamako, the capital of the Mali Republic, and from there to head across the Sahara by way of the desert outpost of Aioun-el-Atrouss to Villa Cisneros on the coast. However the French official who operated the small airstrip at Man told us that he could not let us take off until we had obtained permission to land at Bamako; and he furthermore thought it doubtful that the ASECNA, the French organization that is responsible for search and rescue in the Sahara, would allow a single-engine aircraft to cross the desert. We were therefore forced to modify our plans and decided instead to head west to the land of President Tubman.

Liberia has been called the only American colony in Africa. In fact it never was a colony and Tubman himself has expressed his regret on this account. Like Freetown, Sierra Leone, and Libreville, Gabon, Liberia came into existence as a settlement for freed slaves. Early in the nineteenth century as public opinion in the United States began to turn against slavery, the problem had arisen of what was to be done with the negroes once they were freed. Many people favoured the idea of shipping them back to Africa where they had come from. (Only in 1962 I heard this very view expressed by a farmer in Virginia, U.S.A.) The number of American slaves resettled in Liberia was probably not great and today only some 15,000 or about 1 per cent of the population are regarded as 'Americo-Liberians', although it is they who monopolize the country's wealth and dominate the government. For more than a century after 1847 when its independence was recognized, Liberia was the only republic on the African continent. It has suffered grievously from poverty, corruption and maladministration; and on occasion the United States has been forced to step in to put its affairs in order. For many years the Americo-Liberians, who had themselves been freed from the bonds of slavery not long before, ruthlessly exploited their fellow negroes of the interior, shipping large numbers as slave-labour to the Spanish island of Fernando Po. And as recently as 1931 an international commission discovered large-scale trafficking in slaves, which Liberian Government officials not only condoned, but profited from.

Today the situation in Liberia is improving. Since the 1920's the country has been largely the preserve of the American Firestone Tire and Rubber Company which obtained the right to lease one million acres of land for rubber plantations. More recently some of the richest iron-ore in the world has come to be mined in the Bomi Hills forty miles inland from the capital, Monrovia. Both these enterprises have done much to set Liberia's economy on its feet.

Approaching Monrovia from the nearby airfield one drives along an ill-paved road littered with garbage and lined on either side by a shanty-town of corrugated-iron shacks. Then from the filth and squalor there rises up a handful of multi-storey air-conditioned prestige buildings; all at once one finds oneself in a world of milk bars and hamburgers, hot dogs and Coca-Cola. At the time of our visit work was in progress on a lavish new building (complete with fall-out shelter) the purpose of which was to enable the President to entertain visiting statesmen in suitable style. The cost of this essential item when it was completed early in 1964 amounted to $20 million—a sum exactly double Liberia's 1953 budget. To a casual observer there might appear to be a certain lack of a sense of priority.

While we were having a look at Monrovia's busy seaport Arnold came across a compatriot of his who was working with a German Forestry Mission which had been sent to Liberia to determine what sort of trees were to be found there and whether they had any commercial value. A few minutes' talk with him gave us some idea of the primitive nature of the country's interior. He told us that the mission had split up into groups and was under-taking a systematic exploration of an area of jungle. The groups break camp at dawn and head through the dense forest hacking a path with machetes and axes as they go. They use compasses and lengths of rope to establish where they are. In the late afternoon, having advanced perhaps a few hundred feet, they pitch camp. As they do so, they clear away an area of jungle around the camp, making a note of the trees and grading them for their quality. The German told us that he was setting out the following morning to join his comrades and he said that we were welcome to come along with him provided we brought our own food and camping equipment. By way of an afterthought he mentioned the fact that the group he was going to join was working five days' march from the nearest road. Had it not been for this and the difficulty of procuring the necessary equipment, we would have been tempted to accept his offer. As it was, with our heads already turned towards home, we decided to push on northwards up the coast.

The tiny West African territory of the Gambia will be Britain's sole remaining colony on the African continent once Southern Rhodesia has become independent. It is no more than a narrow enclave that follows the course of the Gambia river some three hundred miles into Senegal and extends five to ten miles on either side of the river. Its population which numbers little over 300,000 depends almost entirely on the groundnut (or peanut) for its livelihood. The reason for the Gambia being last in the queue for independence seems to be the fact that the Gambians themselves have so far shown little interest in joining the queue. Unlike the larger and more prosperous states of Africa, there has arisen in the Gambia no vociferous nationalist movement. As a result one is presented with the strange spectacle of a colonial power actually having to encourage a colony to take its independence. The British Governor Sir John Paul told me almost plaintively how, on his recent arrival in the colony, instead of being met with demands for independence and shouts of 'Limey Go Home', he had been greeted by a cheering crowd and a flutter of Union Jacks. The Gambians are a happy people but they seem to care little for politics—perhaps this is the cause of their happiness. The political whirlwind has not yet struck the Gambia, or it might be more correct to say that it has not yet been stirred up by her politicians.

Elsewhere on the continent, politicians have had everything to gain by teaching their peoples the precept that 'Man lives not by bread alone . . .' but this has not been the case in the Gambia where there is a considerable likelihood that after independence the territory will become part of French-speaking Senegal which surrounds it on all sides. If this were to happen the English-speaking Gambian politicians would soon find themselves out of a job; it is perhaps this thought in the back of their minds that has made them rather dilatory in arousing the political awareness of their people and demanding independence.

From the small capital town of Bathurst that stands on the mouth of the Gambia River we headed inland. Both Arnold and I were anxious to make one last hop into the interior before the end of the trip, and during our brief stay in Bathurst we had dis-cussed the possibilities with the Governor, who kindly offered to arrange for us to visit the town of Basse that lies on the river some 250 miles upstream. He told us that there was nowhere at Basse itself where we could land our aircraft, but said that if we followed a track that led south from there into Senegal for about ten miles we would find a small landing-strip at a village called Wellingera where he would have us met. Since the village was not marked on our map, we contacted Dakar on the H.F. radio as soon as we were airborne to obtain confirmation of its position by co-ordinates of latitude and longitude. It was several minutes before a reply was forthcoming and when it was, it put the position of Wellingera 105 miles north of Basse, instead of ten miles south as we had been told by the Governor. When we asked the Dakar controller if he would mind checking his figures, he retorted with a demand to know whether we had landing permission for Senegal. Thereupon Arnold put on his most authoritative voice and declared: 'This flight has diplomatic clearance.' With this the controller seemed impressed and we heard no more. We continued on our way inland flying only a few feet above the surface of the river in the hope of seeing some crocodiles.

We reached Basse after an hour's flight and turned south as instructed by the Governor. The parched ground beneath us was dotted here and there with scrub-bush and we soon lost sight of the track we were supposed to follow. Just as we were becoming rather apprehensive of our chances of finding the airstrip, we suddenly saw standing in the bush ahead what looked like an enormous white elephant. As we approached we could hardly believe our eyes. There before us, near a collection of grass-huts, was drawn up a gleaming white Rolls Royce; beside it lay a short dirt runway. We had to overshoot on our first approach when we saw a herd of goats wandering across the runway. However the valiant efforts of a Senegalese gendarme soon drove them off and we were able to come in to land the second time around. All the village of Wellingera had turned out to watch our arrival and we soon found ourselves surrounded by an excited throng of people. It was only with difficulty that we were able to manœuvre the Comanche to the edge of the runway and park it beside the Rolls Royce, which turned out to be the property of the Basse District Commissioner Mr Gordon Edwards who had come to meet us. An air-conditioned Rolls Royce (complete with record-player) is one of the last things one would expect to see in the backwoods of Africa where there is not a paved road for miles around. Another is an iced bottle of champagne. Yet to our amazement, before we had been on the ground five minutes in this small grass-hut village in Senegal we found ourselves seated in a Rolls Royce clasping a sweating bottle of champagne which the local Senegalese Prefect had generously presented to us, insisting: 'I know you English like this stuff.' This was not the first time we had been put to shame by the remarkable generosity of Africans we had met on our trip, and we much regretted having nothing to give in return.

Basse, a small trading centre standing on the banks of the Gambia River, is two towns in one. For four months of the year, during the rainy season that lasts from June until October, half the town is completely submerged beneath the river's flood-waters. When this happens all the inhabitants retreat to higher ground nearby where they have built alternative accommodation for themselves. We arrived in the middle of the dry season and the small houses and trading stores in the more elevated part of town were boarded up and abandoned. All activity had been transferred to other buildings beside the river. At the time of our visit the government was about to embark on the almost im-possible task of conducting a census. Some posters had been printed to announce the fact, and to advise the people: 'If you do not know how old you are, ask the elders of your tribe.' As we wandered around the town we came across the citizen who had been entrusted with the task of sticking up the posters; he was proudly admiring a smart-looking poster that he had just finished putting up. When we pointed out that it was upside down, he explained, as might any critic of modern art, that he thought it looked better the other way up. The passers-by evidently agreed with him for while casting approving glances at the shiny new poster, none of them seemed to have noticed anything amiss.

We stayed overnight in Basse where the District Commissioner kindly put us up at his house. The following morning we returned to the airfield at Wellingera and took off for Mauretania. We flew over the rough bush and scrub-grass of Senegal's interior for some two hundred miles until we reached the broad flood of the Senegal River and crossed into Mauretania. Thereafter all was desert: nothing but a boundless shimmering sand-sea lay beneath us. As we headed north into the Sahara towards the small desert fortress of Boutilimit, we maintained a strict radio-silence. We knew from our experience the day before that if we contacted Dakar Radio, as by rights we should have done, we would be assailed with a barrage of questions about our failure to obtain either overflying or landing permission for Mauretania. And we did not fancy the possibility of being required to alter course and fly to Dakar where we would find ourselves enmeshed in the red tape of officialdom. We had already had difficulties with the ASECNA on the Ivory Coast where we had been prevented from taking off for Mali without the requisite permission which it would have taken several days to obtain. To avoid being stuck in Dakar and having our freedom of movement thereafter circumscribed by the (rightly) strict regulations governing flights across the Sahara, we decided it was preferable not to announce our flight to the authorities. On the other hand we were equally anxious to avoid being stuck in the middle of the desert in the event of something going wrong. We had therefore made an arrangement with a pilot we had met at Bathurst the previous morning; and before leaving Basse we had contacted him by means of the very efficient V.H.F. radio-telephone system that had recently been established in the Gambia. We gave him the details of our flight as well as our proposed take-off time of noon and we told him we would report when we were overhead Boutilimit which we code-named 'Bravo'. Once north of the Senegal River there were no more landmarks; we had only the St Louis radio-beacon, more than 100 miles away on the coast, to assist our navigation. Nevertheless in the dry desert air we were receiving the radio impulses loud and clear, and we had no difficulty in finding the fortress of Boutilimit, set among the sand dunes that stretched as far as the eye could see. Nearby, we saw a flat strip of sand marked out as a landing area and we radioed our friend in Bathurst: 'Landing Bravo 1355' (1.55 p.m. G.M.T.).

As the propeller swung to a standstill, I opened the cabin door and was struck by a blast of hot air as if from a furnace. I quickly slammed it closed once more. Having landed in Mauretania without visas or permission of any kind, we waited to see what would happen next. After three or four minutes we saw a Land Rover approaching in a cloud of dust from the direction of the fort. It drew up alongside and two men got out. One, who was brown-skinned and wearing a revolver on his belt, was evidently a Moorish gendarme; the other was a young Frenchman. We explained we were on our way to Nouakchott, the Mauretanian capital, and had just dropped in for a quick look around. They were evidently not accustomed to having tourists but they did not seem to take exception to our unannounced arrival. The Frenchman, indeed, appeared delighted to see some new faces. As he drove us back to the fort he explained that he was a doctor employed by the French Government and assigned to Mauretania as part of a technical assistance programme. He added that he and his wife were the only Europeans in Boutilimit and after being there for the previous six months they were somewhat fed up with the place. One had to agree the amenities were not very extensive. The outpost consisted of no more than a settlement of black nomad tents crowded around the fort that stands on top of a sand dune. The only shade was provided by a dozen or so thorn trees; little else can stand the heat and the intense aridity of the air. Life at Boutilimit is sustained by a single well, sunk deep into the sand. The water is hoisted to the surface in a goat-skin tied to the end of a 200 ft rope. The other end of the rope is attached to a donkey which brings the water up as it is driven away from the well. The fort itself was abandoned, except for a few rooms used by the French doctor and his wife. The courtyard was buried under several feet of rich yellow sand. It is a silent place. There is nothing to be heard but the moaning of the wind—a hot, dry dusty wind that has travelled perhaps 3,000 miles or more across the burning Sahara. Now and then it lifts a cloud of fine sand into the air, blinding and suffocating man and beast. This is indeed the wilderness—a wilderness that destroys the living, yet preserves the dead.

After a much needed drink with the doctor and his wife, we returned to the aircraft and took off for the coast. We had to land at Nouakchott in order to refuel before going on to the Canary Islands where we planned to make a night landing that evening. However we found Nouakchott Airport deserted, and it was several minutes before the French airport manager arrived in a *deux-chevaux* Citroën to tell us that we could not have fuel as it was Sunday and the airport was closed. He said we would have to wait until the following morning and suggested that it might be a good idea if before we took off we obtained landing permission from the Director of Civil Aviation.

By this stage of the journey our letters of introduction had just about run out; we therefore set about finding a British Embassy or Consulate. However it soon transpired that the nearest one was in Dakar, more than 250 miles away. In the days when Mauretania was a French colony it was administered from Senegal. And only since it became independent in 1960 has a new capital been built at Nouakchott where the sands of the Sahara reach to the very brink of the ocean and are pounded by the giant Atlantic rollers. Mauretania is one of the most desolate countries in the world: it has an area more than six times greater than England, but its population is less than one sixtieth the size. The capital itself consists of little more than a handful of modern official buildings set among the dunes. Sand is everywhere. At the time of our visit Nouakchott's first surfaced road had not yet been completed. It is perhaps hardly surprising that foreign countries have been slow in establishing embassies in the new capital. One of the few countries to have done so is the United States. Arnold and I therefore decided to try our luck by ringing the door-bell of the new gleaming white single-storey building. After a while the door was opened by the Embassy's second secretary Mr Richard Dawson who appeared in his dressing-gown having evidently been aroused from his siesta. He invited us in and we explained our predicament in air-conditioned comfort.

As luck would have it he had just started to learn to fly with the local flying club and he knew the Director of Civil Aviation. Better still, he invited us to dinner and offered us a couple of beds for the night—an offer we were not slow to accept. That evening we had a very pleasant dinner with the chargé d'affaires and the rest of the Embassy staff at a small French restaurant. None of them had passed their middle thirties and they seemed very much the New Frontier type. After dinner everyone engaged in a monkey hunt along the beach to recover a pet lost by one of the chargé d'affaires' children.

The following morning Richard Dawson accompanied us to the Director of Civil Aviation, an amiable Spaniard with a long beard, long hair and long black baggy trousers that are the fashion in the Sahara. In no time at all he had given us the necessary landing permission and overflying permission. When I asked him if we would have any difficulty with the ASECNA in being allowed to fly direct to Villa Cisneros and from there head straight out across the Atlantic to the Canary Islands, he declared with the authority worthy of a general: 'Ici, l'ASECNA c'est moi!' And he told us we could go right ahead.

After thanking our hosts of the night before, we refuelled the Comanche and took off for the Canary Islands. We flew up across the western Sahara for nearly two and a half hours before overflying Villa Cisneros and striking out across the ocean towards the island of Tenerife more than 300 miles away. When we had made the short sea-crossing from England to France at the beginning of our flight, we had listened with apprehension to the engine's every vibration. Now however, we had such confidence in our Comanche and its powerful Lycoming engine that we did not think twice about a two-hour flight over water in an area little frequented by shipping. We were still 200 miles away from Tenerife when we saw the island's 12,000 ft snow-crested volcano rising out of the deep blue waters of the Atlantic. The idea of seeing snow after the miles of scorching desert we had overflown, seemed incredible. At Nouakchott Airport that morning the thermometer on our windscreen had registered 115° F. When we touched down at Tenerife four and a half hours later the temperature was a chilly 58°, yet Arnold's aunt and uncle who had just arrived there from ice-bound Europe were remarking how warm it was.

Tenerife is the most spectacular of Spain's Canary Islands and we spent three enjoyable and relaxing days there staying with some friends of Arnold's who had a tomato-farm on the southern end of the island. We then headed north-east to Morocco and made a night-stop at Marrakesh which lies in a plain at the foot of the snow-shrouded Atlas Mountains. The next day we flew on to Fez where we spent the morning exploring the dark and narrow alleys of the ancient city. When we returned to the nearby airport after lunch, we found a large military band drawn up beside our aircraft. Since this was not an every day occurrence we got out our cameras to take a photograph. But before we had time to do so we were pounced upon by four Moroccan soldiers. A young officer appeared and demanded to see our papers. Arnold produced his passport: it was promptly confiscated. Mine was in the aircraft only ten yards away but when I offered to go and fetch it I was told to stay where I was. The officer then asked me my name. I told him. He thereupon pronounced me drunk and ordered a soldier to arrest both of us. We were forthwith removed to a nearby grass verge where we were held under guard. It was of no avail explaining that we were pilots and that all we wanted to do was to make a flight-plan and get on our way. It was a most uncomfortable feeling to find oneself detained for no reason at all by a junior officer of a foreign army, without anyone knowing where one was. We learned from our guard, who was rather more civil than the officer, that the large body of soldiers was at the airport for the departure of Signor Segni, the Italian President, who was in Morocco for a state visit. Nearly two hours passed before the Italian President's aircraft took off and even then we were not released. I demanded to see the officer but was told that he was busy. Seeing him standing not far away I marched over towards him, but before I reached him half a dozen soldiers were on to me. It was only when the time came for the troops to return to their barracks that we were with ill-grace released. Our guard who spoke excellent French was very apologetic about the behaviour of his officer. 'You must understand,' he pleaded, 'this is not a European army. Here everyone gives orders and no one knows what is going on.'

It was nearly dusk when we touched down at Tangier and a cold fog was rolling in from the sea. The town, contrary to our expectations, was grey, dismal and deserted. We determined to make an early start and do our best to cover the 1,200 miles from Africa to England the next day.

Low cloud delayed our departure the following morning and it was not until 8.25 a.m. that we were airborne. The weather over Spain was bad and we were forced to climb to 15,000 ft to keep clear of the worst of the cloud. However Biarritz was clear, and we landed there just before noon to refuel. From there we flew up across France and the English Channel to Hurn in southern England where we cleared Customs and refuelled a second time. We reached Oxford by 5 p.m. Everyone there seemed surprised to see us; they were even more surprised to see the Comanche back without so much as a scratch after its 20,000 mile safari. My instructor Jeremy Busby rubbed his eyes and heaved a deep sigh of relief. He climbed aboard with us and we took off for Boxted, a disused airfield near my father's house in Suffolk. It was already half an hour after sunset when we came in to land at Boxted. My father was at the end of the runway with his car head-lights on to guide us in. And we touched down with the aid of our landing-lights at 6.25 p.m. just ten hours after leaving the shores of Africa. As the roar of the engine died, my father greeted us with the words: 'I have killed the fatted calf.' For the home-coming of the prodigal son?

INDEX

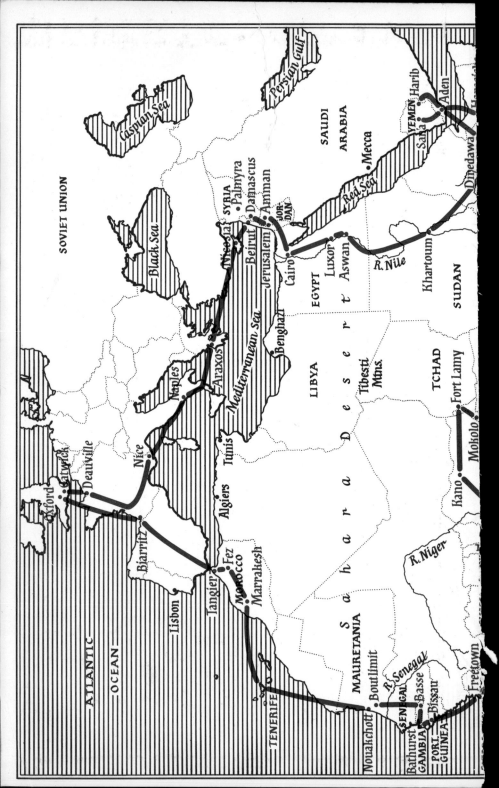